I0794458

HOFSTRA ATHLETICS

FRONT COVER: Howard "Howdy" Myers served as Hofstra University's director of athletics, head men's lacrosse coach, and football coach for a quarter of a century. Myers is credited with the tremendous growth of lacrosse on Long Island, through the creation of scholastic clinics and demonstrations in the 1950s, and leading the Hofstra lacrosse program to national prominence. (Courtesy of Hofstra University Archives/Athletic Communications.)

COVER BACKGROUND: The image depicts the first women's team in Hofstra sports history. The field hockey team dates back to the 1936 season. Hofstra finished 2-5-1 in its inaugural season under head coach Erma Stroh. Interestingly, five of the eight games were played against local high schools. The team earned its wins against Northport High School and Nassau Collegiate Center in the final two contests of the year. (Courtesy of Hofstra University Archives/Athletic Communications.)

BACK COVER: The jersey numbers of 25 student-athletes from Hofstra's sports history have been retired in recent years. This image shows the jerseys of five men's basketball players at Hofstra hanging in the rafters of the David S. Mack Sports and Exhibition Complex. In order, the jerseys belong to Bill Thieben, Steve Nisenson, Rich Laurel, Speedy Claxton, and Charles Jenkins. (Courtesy of Len Skoros/Hofstra.)

HOFSTRA ATHLETICS

Chris R. Vaccaro
Foreword by Craig "Speedy" Claxton

ARCADIA PUBLISHING

Copyright © 2011 by Chris R. Vaccaro
ISBN 978-0-7385-7664-0

Published by Arcadia Publishing
Charleston, South Carolina

Printed in the United States of America

Library of Congress Control Number: 2011932031

For all general information, please contact Arcadia Publishing:
Telephone 843-853-2070
Fax 843-853-0044
E-mail sales@arcadiapublishing.com
For customer service and orders:
Toll-Free 1-888-313-2665

Visit us on the Internet at www.arcadiapublishing.com

To all of the former and current Hofstra University student-athletes, coaches, professors, and administrators who have made the university what it is today.

CONTENTS

FOREWORD

There are few views more spectacular than standing on top of a stepladder looking out over a sea of fans on the basketball court celebrating a championship you have spent the last four years of your life building towards (see image on page 86).

I was fortunate enough to have that experience my senior year at Hofstra University as our team defeated the University of Delaware, 76-69, in the America East championship game on March 11, 2000. To this day it ranks as one of the greatest moments of my athletic career.

What made it even more special was that we won the championship on our home floor, and when I climbed the ladder, I was able to look out at all the members of the Hofstra community who had supported our program throughout my career.

It is that community that has helped Hofstra University grow into the thriving academic and athletic institution it is today.

The 1999–2000 basketball season marked the first-ever in the David S. Mack Sports and Exhibition Complex, and in the short 11 years since the Mack Sports Complex was built, this university has grown in so many different ways. Most recently, the university added the Hofstra North Shore-LIJ School of Medicine that will enhance its already stellar academic reputation.

Many Hofstra graduates have left their mark in various professional fields. This list includes educators, business leaders, actors, politicians, members of the medical community, and athletes. I am fortunate to share that stage with numerous former student-athletes who have gone on to greatness in the field of athletics. From Wayne Chrebet to Marques Colston to Danielle Stewart (first-ever Olympic medalist), this list is growing by the year and 2010 Hofstra graduate Charles Jenkins is next in line to carry the Hofstra banner into the National Basketball Association (NBA) with the Golden State Warriors.

I am happy to share this book with you. As a fellow graduate of Hofstra University, Chris Vaccaro has the same love and appreciation for Hofstra that I do, and through the pictures and captions on the following pages, he has done a wonderful job telling the story of Hofstra Athletics.

Thank you and Go Pride!

—Craig "Speedy" Claxton
Class of 2000

ACKNOWLEDGMENTS

This book, like all others, would not have been possible without the support of many people.

I would like to thank Hofstra president Stuart Rabinowitz and Hofstra student-athletes, coaches, and administrators, past and present, for their contributions to Hofstra Athletics.

The following individuals also were instrumental in the construction of this book: Brian Ballweg, Hofstra photographer; Geri Solomon, Barbara Guzowski, and Hofstra University Archives; Jack Hayes, Hofstra director of athletics; Melissa Connolly, Hofstra vice president for university relations; Stephen Gorchov, Hofstra associate director of athletics for communications; Len Skoros, Hofstra director of athletic publications; Jim Sheehan, Hofstra senior sports information director; and Jeremy Kniffin.

The following photographers have photographs which appear in this book: Brian Ballweg, Scott Bruhn, Lawrence French, Jeff Golden, Howard Gorchov, Jeff Jacobsen, Ross Obley, Dave Olds, Jorge Perez, Joe Rogate, Joe Rokita, Stephen Slade, Ben Solomon, David Gonzales, Alex Trautwig, Brian Westerholt, and Darl Zehr. The following organizations also have photographs in this book: New York Jets, Indiana Pacers, Colonial Athletic Association, University of Delaware, University of Maryland, Marshall University, University of Notre Dame, and News 12.

I have to thank my family and friends for their undying support in all of my journalistic efforts.

Lastly, but certainly not least, thank you to the wonderful people at Arcadia Publishing who have been professional and enjoyable to work with throughout the course of both books I have had published through their fine company.

I strove to pack as many influential figures and photographs into this text as possible, but space restraints hinder the number of images that can be used in the final product. There are many more athletes and coaches in the last 75 years who have helped make Hofstra what it is today, and they will always be remembered.

INTRODUCTION

During the 2010–2011 men's basketball season at Hofstra University, Charles Jenkins garnered as much media attention as any college athlete in the tristate area. He finished his career as the all-time leading scorer in school history, one of the best to ever perform in the Colonial Athletic Association, and followed that by being the first active player at Hofstra to have his jersey number retired (No. 22) and be drafted by the NBA's Golden State Warriors.

A common theme, however, in the media coverage outside of the traditional New York papers and websites always mentioned Hofstra as a small school; a mid-major-type athletic program with sparks of glory over the years, annunciating a hidden gem always shining. In reality, though, Hofstra, which has existed for more than 75 years since its inception as a small commuter school in 1935, has become an internationally recognized institution for its academic and athletic success. With 115 buildings; 12,000 students enrolled in undergraduate, graduate, law, and medical school courses; and its accreditation as an arboretum, the school, located in Hempstead, New York, on Long Island, is a major cultural institution on an ever-evolving island and has produced some of the finest students in the nation.

The same can be said for its athletic program, which has seen some of its most productive seasons in the last two decades in school history. From former Hofstra athletes who have won Super Bowls or NBA championships to the plethora of professional athletes who have represented the university with pride, there has been a long list of accolades involving the Hofstra athletic program.

Long before Charles Jenkins completed his due diligence in keeping Hofstra on the map, players—like John Schmitt, who won a Super Bowl with the New York Jets; Bill Thieben, who played in the NBA for the Fort Wayne Pistons; and Wayne Chrebet, who became a New York fan-favorite with the Jets—all did their part in making the Hofstra name mean something. Others followed suit like Doug Shanahan, the inaugural Tewaaraton Award winner as the nation's top lacrosse player in 2001; Marques Colston and Willie Colon, who won the Super Bowl with the New Orleans Saints and Pittsburgh Steelers, respectively; and athletes like Tiffany Yovino, a soccer phenom who was the school's first athlete to ever be nominated for NCAA Woman of the Year. Along with thousands of other athletes who wore the Hofstra name on their chest over the last 75-plus years, they have all attempted and succeeded at making their time at Hofstra mean something.

Along with growth in conference status came the addition and development of two decades worth of capital projects that aided in the profile and characterization of the university you see today. With the help of generous members of the Hofstra community, the university has first-class facilities across its campus.

Still, Hofstra athletics would not be what it is today without coaching staffs and administrative figures that helped craft and mold the athletic culture that has lasted more than 75 years. Names like Jack MacDonald, James M. Shuart, Howdy Myers, Nathalie J. Smith, Harry Royle, Sylvia J.

Giallombardo, and Joe Gardi are synonymous with winning and legendary status and laid the foundation for the future of the program. Creating a winning culture allowed for the university's first nationally televised game in March 2000 when Hofstra beat Delaware in the America East Conference men's basketball championship. Eventually the wrestling and lacrosse programs would appear on national television as well. And then programs started beating No. 1 ranked schools and defending national champions when softball topped UCLA, men's lacrosse beat Johns Hopkins, and wrestling knocked off Minnesota. The renowned coaches—ones like Myers, Bill Edwards and Fran Kalafer, who are recognized as national hall of fame coaches in their respective sports—have left an indelible mark on their athletes and the institution.

Formerly known as the Flying Dutchmen, Hofstra changed its moniker to the Pride in 2004. Hofstra competes at the NCAA Division I level and is a member of the Colonial Athletic Association. With 17 varsity sports on campus, the amount of history and memories collected since the school's inception is insurmountable. In recent years the university has harnessed a respect for the legends who made Hofstra what it is today and have retired the jersey numbers of 25 athletes.

One of the great features of the university is its ability to adapt and grow but to maintain a sense of tradition. It is obvious when you walk around campus and see the jersey numbers hanging at various facilities, when you walk into Margiotta Hall and see the second floor covered with historical-themed walls, or when you walk into the arena at the David S. Mack Sports and Exhibition Complex and see the walls covered in basketball history. It is everywhere, and it is hard to miss. The Pride faithful have done an extraordinary job both making and recreating history.

1

1930s–1940s

JACK MACDONALD. Jack MacDonald served as Hofstra's first director of athletics from 1937 to 1942 and later from 1945 to 1948, as well as the school's first football, basketball, and baseball coach. In six seasons, from 1936 to 1941 and in 1946, MacDonald compiled a 21-17-1 record as football coach. In basketball, he was 90-52 through seven seasons, which came in two stints from 1936 to 1942 and 1946 to 1947. He coached baseball from 1938 to 1942 and compiled a record 30-17-1. (Courtesy of Hofstra University Archives/ Athletic Communications.)

HOFSTRA'S FIRST FOOTBALL FIELD. The field in this photograph, which was located on the far end of the south side of campus, looks much different than James M. Shuart Stadium where the football team played in the modern era. This photograph was taken in the 1930s when the football program began. Hofstra was 8-9-1 in that decade, fielding its first team in 1937. (Courtesy of Hofstra University Archives/Athletic Communications.)

HOFSTRA'S FIRST TENNIS TEAM. In 1938, Hofstra's first tennis team took to the court. Sporting sweaters with a bold "H" to represent Long Island's newest college, the women's tennis program has existed since that season. Hofstra's athletic program grew exponentially in the late 1930s, adding numerous sports in a short period of time. (Courtesy of Hofstra University Archives/Athletic Communications.)

WOMEN'S BASKETBALL, 1936–1937. The Hofstra women's basketball program was established in 1936 and put together an 11-4-1 season out of the gate under head coach Erma Stroh. Like the field hockey program at the time, also coached by Stroh, many of the games the basketball team played were against local high schools. But Hofstra faced William & Mary that season, resulting in a 14-14 tie. The Tribe ranks as the Pride's oldest current rival. (Courtesy of Hofstra University Archives/Athletic Communications.)

HOFSTRA BASEBALL, 1941. This action shot is one of the oldest baseball photographs the university has in its archives. The program started in 1937 and was coached by Jack MacDonald from 1938 to 1942. In 1941, when this photograph was taken, Hofstra was 5-3. Most of the school's competition came from the tristate area with schools like NYU and CCNY being on the schedule consistently for the first couple of decades in program history. From 1944 to 1946, there was no baseball, as was the case with most sports on campus, because of World War II. (Courtesy of Hofstra University Archives/Athletic Communications.)

HOFSTRA WRESTLING, 1948–1949. Wrestling started a year before this photograph was taken during the 1948–1949 season. Walter "Brick" Stone was the first head coach and stayed at the helm from 1947 to 1960. At the NCAA championships in 1948, Hofstra was well represented. Phil Gunther charged his way to the consolation semifinals but lost to Arthur Archer from Illinois. Francis Fusco also made it to the consolation quarterfinals that season. (Courtesy of Hofstra University Archives/Athletic Communications.)

HOFSTRA FOOTBALL, 1940. This classic shot is of the Hofstra football team from 1940. That season, under Jack MacDonald, Hofstra was 4-3 and captained by Phil Musa and John Nastronero. The team averaged 21 points per game compared to its opponents, which put up 10.4 points per contest. (Courtesy of Hofstra University Archives/Athletic Communications.)

HOFSTRA MEN'S BASKETBALL, 1940–1941. Hofstra strung together a 13-7 record during the 1940–1941 season. Its largest winning streak hit seven games towards the second half of the year. They played familiar schools, such as St. John's, Pace, and St. Francis at the time, but also other opponents that are either in different levels of NCAA play or defunct today, like Plattsburgh, Lowell Textile, and NY Agriculture. (Courtesy of Hofstra University Archives/Athletic Communications.)

THE BLUE BEETLE. For on-campus transportation, students for more than 70 years have used the Blue Beetle to get around. This fun photograph from 1937 shows the women's basketball team in the original Blue Beetle bus. Today, the university's athletic teams travel to road games via private charter airplanes, commercial airlines, and coach buses equipped with the latest technology. (Courtesy of Hofstra University Archives/Athletic Communications.)

Calkins Gymnasium. Calkins Hall was originally known as Calkins Gymnasium in the 1940s and, as seen in this picture, was the original home of the men's and women's basketball teams. A member of the basketball team from the 1940s is shown driving to the basket at Calkins in front of a packed house. (Courtesy of Hofstra University Archives/ Athletic Communications.)

Hofstra Baseball, 1940s. This rare action shot from Hofstra's archives shows an athlete trying to beat out a play at first base during a game against an unknown opponent. The photograph is indicative of the times from the older model cars and buildings in the background as well as the uniform he is sporting. (Courtesy of Hofstra University Archives/ Athletic Communications.)

JACK SMITH. Serving as the second baseball coach in school history from 1943 to 1962, Jack Smith is still the program's all-time leader in wins with 179. His winning percentage of .560 is second to Jack MacDonald, who only coached the sport for five seasons. Smith also coached basketball from 1943 to 1946 and football from 1947 to 1949. (Courtesy of Hofstra University Archives/Athletic Communications.)

ROBERT "RED" BENN, 1940. Red Benn is one of the most recognizable figures from Hofstra's baseball program in the early days. He graduated from the school in 1940 and also played football and basketball. Benn was an All-Met Conference selection on the diamond and helped the baseball team to a 12-3 record in his final season (1940). (Courtesy of Hofstra University Archives/Athletic Communications.)

HOFSTRA MEN'S BASKETBALL, 1940S. This photograph, taken in the early 1940s, shows Frank Reilly, Harry Yale, Lou Buffolino, and Richard Peterman. They all graduated from Hofstra in 1941 and played for Jack MacDonald. (Courtesy of Hofstra University Archives/Athletic Communications.)

WALTER "BRICK" STONE. Brick Stone, a longtime coach and administrator, served Hofstra from 1946 through 1978. He was a founder of the wrestling program and helped the sport grow on Long Island. Stone coached the wrestling, cross country, and track and field teams and posted a 77-53-10 record in 13 seasons with the wrestling team (1947–1960). Stone, a Long Island native who ran track and played football at Michigan, was inducted posthumously into the National Wrestling Hall of Fame in 2005. (Courtesy of Hofstra University Archives/Athletic Communications.

2

1950s–1960s

Howard "Howdy" Myers. Howdy Myers was the football (1950–1974) and lacrosse (1950–1975) coach and served as director of athletics (1951–1974) at Hofstra for more than 20 years. As lacrosse coach, Myers recorded a 214-139-4 record. He coached eight divisional championship teams and made four NCAA tournament appearances. In 1971, he was inducted into the US Lacrosse Hall of Fame. As football coach, he compiled a 141-98-4 record, and the 1959 squad went 9-0 and was the first undefeated team in program history. (Courtesy of Hofstra University Archives/ Athletic Communications.)

Ed Gaffney, 1971. Ed Gaffney played soccer at Hofstra in 1968 and 1969 and was the first All-American in program history. He came to Hofstra in 1968 after six months at the US Merchant Marine Academy and immediately made his mark as he helped Hofstra to its first NCAA tournament appearance that season, scoring a school record 19 goals in pacing the Pride to a 15-2-1 record. In 1969, he continued his scoring prowess with 18 goals and was named to the Honorable Mention All-America team. (Courtesy of Hofstra University Archives/ Athletic Communications.)

Marty Willigan, 1969. Marty Willigan, Hofstra's first two-time All-American in wrestling, was a two-time NCAA qualifier and a two-time conference champion. Willigan placed fourth at the NCAA championships in 1968 and second in 1969, losing to Dan Gable in the finals. Following graduation from Hofstra, he was a member of the USA Wrestling Team at the World Games for the Deaf and won two gold medals. (Courtesy of Hofstra University Archives/ Athletic Communications.)

BILL THIEBEN, 1956. One of the most dominating players of his era, Bill Thieben scored 2,045 points and grabbed 1,837 rebounds during his 76-game, three-year career. He is Hofstra's career leader in rebounds and ranks in the top 10 in career scoring. An All-American at Hofstra, Thieben was selected by the Fort Wayne Pistons of the NBA in the 1956 draft, and he played with the Pistons from 1956 to 1958, seeing action in 85 games. (Courtesy of Hofstra University Archives/ Athletic Communications.)

STEVE NISENSON, 1966. Steve Nisenson left Hofstra as the school's all-time leading scorer with 2,222 points, a record that stood for 43 years. He led the team in scoring in each of his three seasons and was a member of two NCAA Division II tournament teams. A two-time All-America selection, he was selected by the New York Knicks in the fifth round of the 1965 NBA draft. (Courtesy of Hofstra University Archives/ Athletic Communications.)

IRVING BURTON, 1952. Irving Burton played baseball and basketball from 1949 to 1952. He was named the 1951 Metropolitan Baseball Conference Most Outstanding Pitcher and set the conference record for strikeouts, and in basketball, he led the team in rebounding for three consecutive seasons. Following graduation, he signed with the New York Giants and played professional baseball for five years. (Courtesy of Hofstra University Archives/Athletic Communications.)

BOB VANDERWARKER. Shown here with Richard Nuttall (left), who took over as the Hofstra men's soccer coach in 1989, Bob Vanderwarker coached the program from 1965 to 1969. His best season came in 1968 when Hofstra finished 15-2-1 and made it to the NCAA tournament for the first time, losing to Fairleigh Dickinson 3-1. Hofstra did, however, beat Temple 3-1 in the MAC championship. Vanderwarker also coached the baseball team at Hofstra from 1966 to 1969 and had a 42-41 record. (Courtesy of Brian Ballweg/Hofstra.)

Jerry Simandl, 1955. Jerry Simandl, an All-American lacrosse player, is one of Hofstra's all-time greats, holding many records that have lasted for more than 50 years, including career points (238), points in a season (102), career assists (119), and assists in a season (58). He played in the annual North-South All-Star game in 1955, and in a *Baltimore Sun* interview with legendary Hofstra coach Howdy Myers conducted in the late 1950s, Simandl was singled out as one of the 10 best players ever coached by Myers. (Courtesy of Hofstra University Archives/Athletic Communications.)

Bill Sanford, 1955. Bill Sanford holds three rushing records at Hofstra: he scored six touchdowns against Wagner in 1952 for a single-game scoring mark, scored 17 touchdowns that year for the single-season record, and his 40 touchdowns from 1951 to 1954 are a career record as well. Sanford was selected in the 27th round of the 1955 NFL draft by the Pittsburgh Steelers. (Courtesy of Hofstra University Archives/Athletic Communications.)

BUTCH VAN BREDA KOLFF. Butch van Breda Kolff, who coached at Hofstra for 13 total seasons over two tenures, recorded an overall record of 215-134 at the university. The 23-1 campaign in 1959–1960 still holds as the best single-season winning percentage in school history. His 215 wins are the most of any Hofstra basketball coach, while his .616 winning percentage is the third-highest mark in program history. He coached Hofstra from 1955 to 1962, and after a long career coaching in the NBA, ABA, and college ranks, returned to coach six more seasons, from 1988 to 1994, before retiring from coaching at the end of the 1993–1994 campaign. He is the first person to have coached both an NCAA Final Four team (Princeton, 1965) and an NBA Finals squad (Los Angeles Lakers, 1968 and 1969) and compiled a professional and collegiate coaching record of 773-585, while coaching such basketball legends as Bill Bradley, Elgin Baylor, Jerry West, Wilt Chamberlain, and Pete Maravich. He played basketball at Princeton and was signed by the New York Knicks, playing four years with the team under legendary coach Joe Lapchick. (Courtesy of Hofstra University Archives/Athletic Communications.)

JOSEPH MARGIOTTA, 1950. Joe Margiotta served as the first president and was a founding member of the Hofstra Pride Club. Established in 1989, the Hofstra Pride Club provides additional financial resources and fan support that is necessary to achieve and sustain success in Division I college athletics. Since its inception, the Hofstra Pride Club has raised more than $15 million to support the Hofstra Athletics Department, including more than $5 million in the five-year period from 2006 to 2011. (Courtesy of Brian Ballweg/Hofstra.)

MICHAEL D'AMATO, 1968. Mike D'Amato played football and lacrosse at Hofstra. In 1968, he was a lacrosse All-American with 34 goals and 15 assists and played in the North-South All-Star game. On the gridiron, he was a defensive back and a kick and punt returner, earning Middle Atlantic Conference All-Star honors in 1966 and 1967. D'Amato was selected by the New York Jets in the 10th round of the 1968 NFL draft and was a member of the 1969 Super Bowl championship team. (Courtesy of New York Jets.)

THE TINY 20. The 1956 Hofstra football team is one of the most storied teams in school history. The team found itself down to just 20 players under head coach Howdy Myers, far below the roster size of most of its opponents. At one point, the team had only 16 healthy players, yet they kept finding ways to win. Led by captains James Condon, Michael Russo, and Warren Tucker, the Flying Dutchmen finished the year 7-3. Dave Provenzano rushed for 793 yards and 10 touchdowns on the year. Hofstra earned a dramatic win over Cortland State along the way, as George Wiemer turned a short pass from quarterback Larry Magilligan with less than two minutes to play into a 51-yard touchdown to give Hofstra a 13-7 win. Don Baldwin intercepted a pass on Cortland State's final possession to seal the win. (Courtesy of Hofstra University Archives/ Athletic Communications.)

Lou DiBlasi, 1961. A football and lacrosse player at Hofstra, Lou DiBlasi was an integral part of the 1956 football team known as the Tiny 20 and later wrote a book about that group with the same title. DiBlasi, who played for legendary Hofstra coach Howdy Myers in both sports and captained the football team in 1960, went on to teach and coach in the Half Hollow Hills School District on Long Island for 28 years. (Courtesy of Hofstra University Archives/Athletic Communications.)

Walter Kohanowich, 1952. Walter Kohanowich (center) was Hofstra's first five-sport athlete, earning letters in football, baseball, track, lacrosse, and wrestling from 1948 through 1952. He was the team's leading rusher in 1951 with more than 900 yards, a number that stood in the top 10 of Hofstra's single-season record books for decades. An All-America selection, he eventually went on to coach freshman football and baseball at Hofstra after graduation. (Courtesy of Hofstra University Archives/Athletic Communications.)

James M. Shuart, 1953. Dr. James M. Shuart was a standout on the football and men's lacrosse teams as well as team captain in both sports. He joined the Hofstra administration as an admissions officer in 1959 and subsequently served in various positions until 1971. Shuart became president of Hofstra University in 1976, a position he held for 25 years before retiring in 2001. In 2002, Hofstra Stadium was renamed James M. Shuart Stadium in recognition of his service to the university. (Courtesy of Hofstra University Archives/ Athletic Communications.)

Al Lahood, 1956. Al Lahood was a four-year letter winner in both football and lacrosse and a highly decorated student-athlete during his tenure at Hofstra. A three-year starter on the offensive and defensive lines, he was named to the 1953 All-America team and was also an honorable mention All-East selection and a Long Island Press All-Star. On the lacrosse field, Lahood was a four-year starter and an honorable mention All-American in 1954 and 1955. He was selected to start in the 1955 North-South All-Star game. (Courtesy of Hofstra University Archives/ Athletic Communications.)

JOHN SCHMITT, 1964. John Schmitt was a three-year letter winner on the football team and also lettered in wrestling and track. An offensive lineman, he received All-America honors in 1963 and one year later was signed by the New York Jets, starting an 11-year National Football League career that was highlighted by a Super Bowl championship in 1969. During his Jets tenure, he earned All-Pro honors in 1968–1969 and Most Valuable Lineman accolades in 1972, and he was a team captain. (Courtesy of New York Jets.)

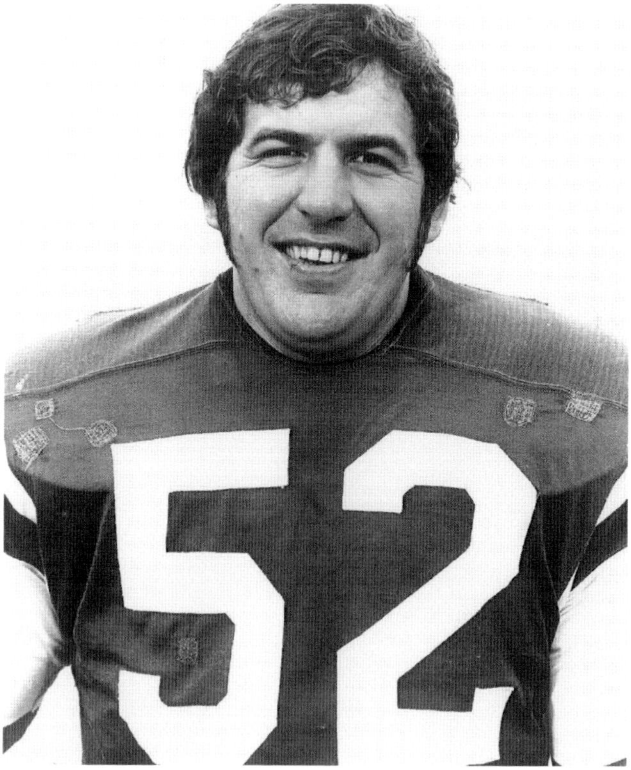

PHIL MORDENTE, 1966. Phil Mordente was a lacrosse standout from 1964 to 1966, recording 211 points, which is second all-time in school history. Mordente earned honorable mention All-America honors in 1965 and was a third team All-American in 1966. He was also named to the North-South All-Star game in 1966. (Courtesy of Hofstra University Archives/Athletic Communications.)

WALTER PETERSEN, 1950. Walter Petersen was a four-sport athlete from 1946 to 1950. An end on both sides of the ball in football, he ranked second on the team in receiving in 1948 with 12 catches for 160 yards. Petersen was a center on the basketball team, a catcher and first baseman on the baseball squad, and excelled at the javelin, shot, and discus in track and field. (Courtesy of Hofstra University Archives/ Athletic Communications.)

HARRY ROYLE, 1970. Harry Royle was Hofstra's director of athletics from 1997 to 2004. After a stellar football career at Hofstra, Royle served as an assistant football coach from 1969 through 1987. He also was an assistant lacrosse coach under Howdy Myers from 1971 through 1975 before replacing the hall of fame coach in 1976, serving as head coach until becoming Hofstra's assistant director of athletics in 1985. (Courtesy of Hofstra University Archives/Athletic Communications.)

3

1970s

Nick Gallo, 1978. Nick Gallo was an NCAA champion at 126 pounds in 1977 and is Hofstra's only wrestling national champion. Gallo was an All-American in 1977 and earned the NCAA Championship Most Outstanding Wrestler Award. During his four-year career at Hofstra, he posted a 104-14 record and earned an alternate position on the 1976 United States Olympic Team. Gallo also coached the Hofstra wrestling team for four years, compiling a 49-25 record with 18 conference champions and 18 NCAA qualifiers. (Courtesy of Hofstra University Archives/Athletics.)

BOB HILLER, 1976. Bob Hiller was a standout lacrosse player for the Pride from 1973 to 1976 and ranks fourth all-time in goals scored with 109. A three-year letterman, he was the team's leading goal scorer in each of his four seasons and was a member of three teams that qualified for the NCAA championship. Each of his teams was ranked in the top 10, including the 1973 team that was ranked fifth in the nation. As a senior in 1976, Hiller was named to the All-America third team. (Courtesy of Brian Ballweg/Hofstra.)

SYLVIA J. GIALLOMBARDO. Dr. Sylvia J. Giallombardo developed the women's athletics program and was the first director of women's athletics at Hofstra, serving in that capacity from 1961 through 1979. As director, she instituted 10 varsity sports for women and introduced volleyball and women's lacrosse as sports in the 1970s. She created the first athletic scholarship program for women and coached the women's basketball team from 1958 to 1974 and served as coach of the softball, tennis, and fencing programs during her tenure as director of women's athletics. (Courtesy of Hofstra University.)

John Irving, 1977. John Irving became the second player in school history to record more than 1,000 rebounds and points after Bill Thieben. Irving scored 1,018 points and grabbed 1,186 rebounds during his three-year career at Hofstra, averaging 13.2 points and 15.4 rebounds per game. His tenure started in Hempstead after transferring from Arizona, where he started at center as a freshman. In 1975–1976, Irving helped Hofstra to its first NCAA Division I tournament appearance. He was selected by the Phoenix Suns in the ninth round of the 1976 NBA draft but opted to return to Hofstra for his senior season and helped the school return to the NCAA tournament. He was a third-round selection of the Detroit Pistons in the 1977 NBA draft. (Courtesy of Brian Ballweg/Hofstra.)

NATHALIE J. SMITH. Dr. Nathalie J. Smith served as head coach of the field hockey, volleyball, and women's lacrosse programs and was chair of the health, physical education, and recreation department as well as an associate professor of physical education. Smith was the first coach of the volleyball club team, which she developed into a varsity program in 1974 and coached for three years. In 1975, she started the women's lacrosse club, which became a varsity sport in 1976, and coached it for five years. (Courtesy of Hofstra University.)

PAUL LYNNER. Paul Lynner spent 10 seasons as the head men's basketball coach at Hofstra, compiling a record of 152-110 and winning percentage of .580. His most successful seasons were his first two, when he went a combined 46-13 in the 1962–1963 and 1963–1964 seasons. Lynner led Hofstra to the NCAA Small College National Tournament in 1963. (Courtesy of Brian Ballweg/Hofstra.)

RICH LAUREL, 1977. Rich Laurel was a four-year letterman on the men's basketball team from 1973 through 1977. He is one of Hofstra's all-time leading scorers with 2,102 points and finished his career with 647 rebounds. He was the 1977 Haggerty Award winner, which is presented to the top player in the New York metropolitan area, and was selected by the Portland Trail Blazers in the first round, 19th overall, of the 1977 NBA draft. Laurel also played professionally in Italy, France, and Belgium. (Courtesy of Brian Ballweg/Hofstra.)

Phil Marino, 1975. Phil Marino, a two-time All-American lacrosse player for the Pride, recorded 26 goals and 31 assists for 57 points in 1975, ranking eighth in the nation in assists and 13th in the nation in overall scoring. He was the MVP of the 1975 USILA North-South All-Star game, the first of three Hofstra players to win the MVP Award, after tallying eight assists in the contest. Marino played for the US World Team in 1978. (Courtesy of Hofstra University.)

Roger Gaeckler. Roger Gaeckler coached the men's basketball team from 1972 to 1979 and had an 85-101 record in seven seasons. He led Hofstra to back-to-back ECC championships in 1976 and 1977, clinching NCAA tournament bids each year. Hofstra lost to Connecticut in overtime 80-78 in the 1976 NCAA tournament and to Notre Dame 90-83 the following season. (Courtesy of Brian Ballweg/Hofstra.)

4

1980s

Hilarie Cranmer, 1989. Dr. Hilarie Cranmer played four years of women's basketball from 1984 to 1988, one year of volleyball, was a two-time Academic All-American, and a 2006 inductee into the CoSIDA Academic All-America Hall of Fame. She currently ranks sixth in scoring in school history with 1,461 points and seventh with 776 rebounds. Cranmer, who received her medical degree from Washington, Missouri, was recognized as the Hofstra legend at the 2006 CAA Women's Basketball Championship. (Courtesy of Brian Ballweg/Hofstra.)

JAMES C. METZGER, 1983. An All-American lacrosse player at both Half Hollow Hills East High School on Long Island and at Hofstra, James C. Metzger led the Flying Dutchmen in assists his freshman and sophomore seasons (1979 and 1980). His single season points per game average (4.9) ranks fifth all-time, and his single season assist average (2.8) ranks eighth. Metzger has been a key benefactor to Hofstra in recent years. (Courtesy of Brian Ballweg/Hofstra.)

DAVID TAYLOR, 1983. David Taylor is the eighth all-time leading scorer in Hofstra men's basketball history with 1,818 points. He also ranks third with 926 career rebounds and second with 178 blocked shots. He led the team in scoring and rebounding averages and field goal percentage all four seasons at Hofstra. (Courtesy of Brian Ballweg/Hofstra.)

Fran Kalafer. An inaugural inductee into the American Volleyball Coaches Association (AVCA) Hall of Fame, Fran Kalafer served as the head volleyball coach at Hofstra from 1981 to 2006. Kalafer closed her 25-year Hofstra coaching career with a record of 590-316 and had a 612-343 overall mark in 28 seasons. During her Hofstra tenure, Kalafer coached five NCAA tournament teams, four National Invitational Volleyball Championship squads, and 14 conference championship teams. The 1995 season was the first of three straight trips to the NCAA tournament, as Kalafer led Hofstra to back-to-back America East titles in 1996 and 1997 and again in 1999. Taking over the reins at Hofstra in 1981, she recorded 22 winning seasons. Kalafer had four teams break the 30-win barrier and 18 teams record at least 20 victories in a season. (Courtesy of Brian Ballweg/Hofstra.)

Leslie Schlegel, 1991. Leslie (Schlegel) Danowski was a dual-sport athlete at Hofstra, lettering in women's basketball and softball and serving as captain for both sports. She also coached the women's basketball team from 1993 to 2001. As a senior in basketball, her 12.4 rebounds per game ranked fifth in the nation and she was named team MVP and Hofstra's Female Athlete of the Year. Schlegel, who played professional basketball in Spain after her Hofstra career, was a pitcher in softball and won 44 games, compiling 231 strikeouts in 79 appearances. (Courtesy of Brian Ballweg/Hofstra.)

HARVEY PYSER. The second longest tenured coach in Hofstra women's basketball history, Harvey Pyser was at the helm of the program from 1977 to 1987. Pyser recorded a program record 162 wins. During the 1981–1982 season, Hofstra recorded a team-high 27 wins and beat Colorado College in the third place game at the AIAW Division II National Championships. A year later, Hofstra became a Division I program in women's basketball. (Courtesy of Brian Ballweg/Hofstra.)

LAURA WALKER, 1983. Laura Walker, arguably the greatest tennis player in Hofstra history, won an Association for Intercollegiate Athletics for Women National Championship in 1982 and is one of only two national champions all-time at Hofstra, joining wrestler Nick Gallo. (Courtesy of Brian Ballweg/Hofstra.)

PETER CAPONE, 1985. Dr. Peter Capone earned All-America accolades in 1983 and again in 1985, finishing as the runner-up at 167 pounds in the 1985 NCAA championships. A two-time East Coast Conference champion, he was named the ECC Championship Most Outstanding Wrestler in 1983 and 1985, and he helped the Pride win the 1983 ECC championship. (Courtesy of Brian Ballweg/Hofstra.)

BRUCE QUINN, 1986. Bruce Quinn, a 1986 graduate, played baseball at Hofstra for four seasons. A successful businessman, he owns the Hagerstown, Maryland, Suns minor league team. The recently constructed baseball press box and seating area were named the Quinn Family Grandstand in appreciation of Quinn's leadership in generating support among baseball alumni in order to have the facility constructed. (Courtesy of Brian Ballweg/Hofstra.)

LIZ IRWIN, 1982. Liz (Irwin) Knauss was a four-year letter winner on the women's basketball team from 1978 through 1982 and the starting shortstop on the softball team from 1979 through 1982. She was a two-time Metropolitan Basketball Conference All-Star, a four-time team MVP, and a three-year team captain. During her basketball career, Hofstra posted a 92-40 record and was Eastern AIAW Division II champions in 1982 as well as New York State AIAW Division I champions and AIAW National Tournament participants. (Courtesy of Brian Ballweg/Hofstra.)

Richard Nuttall. Richard Nuttall, the longest current tenured coach at Hofstra, has been at the helm of the men's soccer program since 1989 and has recorded more than 200 career victories. He led Hofstra to three straight Colonial Athletic Association titles from 2004 to 2006 and a pair of NCAA tournament victories. Nuttall played professionally in England and for the Long Island Rough Riders. (Courtesy of Brian Ballweg/Hofstra.)

Bill Siegel, 1980. Bill Siegel played tennis at Hofstra from 1978 through 1980. As a senior in 1980, he was the first Hofstra player to win the East Coast Conference championship in both singles and doubles. He also won the Rider Invitational, was a Metropolitan Collegiate Conference finalist, and went 26-1 on the season. Siegel played professional tennis on the ATP Tour from 1980 to 1984 and became the first Hofstra player to earn an ATP world ranking in singles and doubles. (Courtesy of Brian Ballweg/Hofstra.)

CARIE BODO, 1988. Carie Bodo coached women's lacrosse at Hofstra from 1988 to 2001. She has the most wins and coached more seasons than any other coach in Hofstra women's lacrosse history. Her most successful season came in 2001 when Hofstra won the America East Conference championship and competed in the NCAA tournament. The Pride finished 16-3 that year and was ranked as high as No. 15 in the nation. She also coached the field hockey team from 1988 to 1996. (Courtesy of Brian Ballweg/Hofstra.)

VINNY SOMBROTTO, 1982. One of the most talented players to ever put on the Hofstra men's lacrosse jersey, Vinny Sombrotto led the team in scoring in 1980 with 54 points and 37 goals. Sombrotto, an All-American in 1980, was a member of the US National Team four times, played professionally for the Long Island Lizards and New York Saints and was elected to the National Lacrosse Hall of Fame and Long Island Lacrosse Hall of Fame. (Courtesy of USA Lacrosse/Hofstra.)

GREG POLLI, 1986. One of the best hitters in Hofstra baseball history, Greg Polli recorded the third-highest single-season batting average in school history (.496) in 1985, earning All-America honors. He followed that up in 1986 with the fourth highest mark at .478. Polli's 14 home runs and 62 RBIs in 1985 are second most in a single season for each statistical category. That same season he had a record slugging percentage of .950. He ranks third in school history with 31 career home runs and sixth with 140 RBIs. (Courtesy of Brian Ballweg/Hofstra.)

SHERYL HALL, 1982. Sheryl Hall ranks 11th in school history with 1,276 career points and sixth with 899 rebounds. Hall was an integral part of the 1981–1982 women's basketball team that won 27 games and beat Colorado College in the third-place game of the Division II national championships. (Courtesy of Brian Ballweg/Hofstra.)

Mickey Kwiatkowski. The fifth head football coach in school history, Mickey Kwiatkowski led Hofstra to five NCAA playoff bids from 1981 through 1989. His 68-27-0 record was the best winning percentage (.716) in program history. Kwiatkowski posted seven winning seasons, including six with eight or more victories, during his nine-year tenure. His 1983 team recorded a 10-0-0 regular season record, was ranked third in the nation, and won the Lambert Bowl, emblematic of eastern football supremacy. (Courtesy of Hofstra.)

Sue Gades, 1986. Sue (Gades) Trommer was a four-year letter winner in volleyball and a four-time All-East Coast Conference selection. Gades earned ECC MVP honors in 1985. Her 33 kills against William & Mary in 1985 and 13 block shots and 24 total blocks against Florida State in 1984 are all school records. Gades also holds single-season records for kills (637 in 1985), kills per set (4.79 in 1985), block solos (171 in 1983), block assists (169 in 1984), and total blocks (307 in 1984). Her 783 career blocks are also a record. (Courtesy of Brian Ballweg/Hofstra.)

CINDY LEWIS, 1979. A former student-athlete and head coach at Hofstra, Cindy Lewis graduated from the university in 1979. A member of the field hockey and women's lacrosse programs during her undergraduate years, Lewis went on to coach both programs as well. Lewis, who currently serves as the senior associate director of athletics at Hofstra, was the honoree at the 2010 Hofstra Pride Golf Classic. (Courtesy of Brian Ballweg/Hofstra.)

JOE FOWLER, 1983. Joe Fowler, who came through Hofstra following his brothers William and Michael, was a men's lacrosse All-American in 1983. He holds the school record with 36 saves against Navy in 1980. (Courtesy of Brian Ballweg/Hofstra.)

Christine Moore, 1988. A three-time All-East Coast Conference selection, Christine (Moore) Newins was the ECC MVP in 1987. She holds a single-match record for most block assists with 15 against Drexel in 1984. Moore ranks third for most service aces in a single season with 95 in 1985 and holds the career service ace record with 268. (Courtesy of Brian Ballweg/Hofstra.)

Shawn Cassidy, 1988. Shawn Cassidy, a team captain and all-conference selection, played soccer for the Flying Dutchmen from 1984 through 1987. He was part of Hofstra's East Coast Conference championship in 1985, which the Flying Dutchmen won 1-0 over Delaware in eight overtimes. The game is the longest in NCAA history (169:50), with the winning goal coming with 10 seconds remaining in the eighth overtime. (Courtesy of Brian Ballweg/Hofstra.)

Jeanne Asper, 1992. Jeanne (Asper) Walsh played volleyball for the Pride from 1988 through 1991 and was a key cog on a team that won 124 matches during her career, the highest four-year total in program history. She compiled 1,115 kills and 532 blocks to go along with a career hitting percentage of .302. A four-time All-East Coast Conference selection, Walsh was the 1988 East Coast Conference Rookie of the Year and then closed her career by earning the 1991 ECC and team MVP awards. (Courtesy of Brian Ballweg/Hofstra.)

John Danowski. John Danowski won 192 games as the men's lacrosse head coach at Hofstra from 1986 to 2006. He was named the USILA Division I Coach of the Year in 1993 and was a four-time conference coach of the year. During his coaching career at Hofstra, he won eight conference titles, earned eight NCAA tournament bids, and garnered 17 national rankings among the top 20 teams in the nation. He later went on to coach at Duke. (Courtesy of Brian Ballweg/Hofstra.)

5

1990s

WAYNE CHREBET, 1995. Wayne Chrebet, one of the most-recognizable figures in school history, was Hofstra's first 1,000-yard receiver in 1994 and set a school record (since broken) with 245 receiving yards in a game at Delaware, while tying Jerry Rice's I-AA record (since broken) for touchdown receptions (five). He finished his career with 150 receptions for 2,297 yards. Chrebet spent 11 years with the New York Jets and ranks second in career receptions with 580 and third in receiving yards with 7,365. (Courtesy of Brian Ballweg/Hofstra.)

EDITH GALLAGHER, 1990. Edith Gallagher was a two-sport athlete in field hockey and softball at Hofstra. She was an honorable mention field hockey All-American in 1989 and ended her career as Hofstra's all-time leader in goals (43), assists (18), and points (103)—marks that have since been passed. In softball, her 14 career triples are second all-time in Hofstra history and her .410 single-season average is the third highest. (Courtesy of Brian Ballweg/Hofstra.)

JIM GARVEY. Jim Garvey served as Hofstra's director of athletics from 1987 to 1997. He hired highly successful football coach Joe Gardi in 1990, hall of fame softball coach Bill Edwards that same year, and men's basketball coach Jay Wright in 1994. Garvey oversaw Hofstra's move from Division I Independent to the North Atlantic Conference in 1994. He was also a college referee in football, basketball, and lacrosse, working four bowl games, three NCAA Basketball Tournaments, and six NCAA Lacrosse championship games. (Courtesy of Brian Ballweg/Hofstra.)

Bill Edwards. Bill Edwards is a National Softball Hall of Fame coach and has spent 22 seasons at Hofstra. Edwards has led Hofstra to the regional finals of the NCAA tournament in the 2004, 2005, 2008, and 2010 seasons and helped the Pride capture a remarkable 11-straight conference tournament titles from 1998 to 2008, which is an NCAA Division I softball record. His career record stands at 806-376-3, ranking him in the top 25 in NCAA history in career winning percentage. Edwards guided Hofstra to a school record-tying 45 wins in 2010, as the team won the CAA regular season title, swept through the CAA tournament, and advanced to the NCAA regional finals with two wins over No. 14 Oklahoma State. Edwards, who has been a part of 22 consecutive winning seasons at Hofstra, coached the Pride to a No. 21 ranking in the final 2004 NCAA Division I Softball Poll, and a No. 20 ranking in the final 1994 poll. Edwards has been named the Regional Coach of the Year 10 times in his career. (Courtesy of Brian Ballweg/Hofstra.)

JoAnne Russell. JoAnne Russell started the Hofstra women's soccer program, guiding it from club status in 1992 to its first varsity season in 1993. She finished her career by leading the Pride to a CAA regular season title in 2003, a regular season co-championship in 2004, and a CAA postseason championship and NCAA bid in 2005. During her tenure, Russell coached one All-American (Sue Weber), 23 all-conference players, four all-rookie team selections, two CAA Defensive Players of the Year (Dolores Deasley and Sue Weber), and three CAA Rookies of the Year (Jacki Pollaro, Marie Curtin, and Edel Malone). In addition, six players (Dolores Deasley, Elaine O'Connor, Becky Wachsberger, Marie Curtin, Kacey O'Driscoll, and Edel Malone) have played on the Irish National Team. A two-time CAA Coach of the Year, Russell guided Hofstra to a 138-88-18 record during her tenure. (Courtesy of Brian Ballweg/Hofstra.)

MICHAEL LACROSSE, 1989. Possibly the most fitting name of any athlete in sports history, Michael LaCrosse set a record that still lives strong today in men's lacrosse history at Hofstra with his 10 goals against Virginia in 1989. That same season he was named East Coast Conference MVP and an All-American. LaCrosse's 3.27 goals-per-game average in 1989 is second all-time in a single season and his 49 goals that year are the third most in a single season in program history. (Courtesy of Brian Ballweg/Hofstra.)

GEORGE TISCHLER, 1991. An All-American, George Tischler led Hofstra in total tackles in 1989 (136) and 1990 (109). The 1990 football season was memorable at Hofstra. It was the 50th season in school history, and the Pride earned its first win in the NCAA playoffs, beating Cortland State 35-9. (Courtesy of Brian Ballweg/Hofstra.)

CRYSTAL BOYD, 1994. Crystal Boyd was a four-year starter at shortstop, earning All-American honors and in 1993 led Hofstra to its first NCAA Softball Tournament appearance. Boyd finished her career as the holder of six single-season records, including a .514 batting average in 1992 that led the nation. She was selected by the Georgia Pride in the now defunct Women's Professional Softball League draft. A fixture in the Hofstra top 10 of every major offensive category, Boyd compiled career numbers of a .431 batting average, 68 doubles, 29 triples, 18 home runs, 144 RBIs, 171 runs scored, and 34 stolen bases. In addition to her All-America accolades, Boyd was a four-time all-region selection, a three-time All-Eastern College Athletic Conference (ECAC) and All-East Coast Conference selection, and a two-time Academic All-American. (Courtesy of Brian Ballweg/Hofstra.)

ROBERTO GITTENS, 2001. Roberto Gittens was a part of some of the best men's basketball teams in Hofstra history. He was a major part of the program in 1999 when Hofstra went to the NIT and also appeared in back-to-back NCAA tournaments in 2000 and 2001. He finished his Hofstra career with 1,240 points. Gittens is tied with two others for having played the most games in program history at 124. He set the record for most free throws attempted in a game when he took 24 against Colgate during the 1997–1998 season and ranks third all-time at Hofstra with 138 blocked shots. (Courtesy of Brian Ballweg/Hofstra.)

KATE GORDON, 1998. Kate (Gordon) Clifford was a forward on the women's basketball team from 1994 to 1998. She finished her career with 1,714 points and 1,031 rebounds—the only player in program history to reach that plateau. Gordon played in 109 games during her four years with 102 starts. She averaged 15.7 points and 9.5 rebounds per game and posted 47 career double-doubles. Gordon also ranks second in program history with 272 steals and fourth with 341 free throws. (Courtesy of Brian Ballweg/Hofstra.)

Stacy Jackson, 1995. A four-year member of the Hofstra softball team, Stacy (Jackson) Jones helped lead the Pride to the NCAA tournament in 1993 and 1995. She was a four-time all-region and All-ECAC selection and a three-time all-conference pick. She graduated as a school record holder in career starts (122), innings pitched (885), victories (96), strikeouts (638), and no-hitters (6). In the single-season record book, Jackson held records for innings pitched (256), victories (26 in 1992 and 1994), strikeouts (175 in 1995), and ERA (0.84 in 1993). (Courtesy of Brian Ballweg/Hofstra.)

Joe Gardi. Joe Gardi was the head football coach at Hofstra from 1990 to 2005. He recorded a 119-62-2 record in 16 seasons, and his win total and .650 winning percentage rank second in Hofstra football coaching history. Under Gardi's guidance, Hofstra made the jump from NCAA Division III in 1990 to I-AA in 1994. He came to Hofstra after five years (1985–1990) as assistant supervisor of officials for the National Football League. Gardi ended his memorable career with a 21-10 victory over No. 7 Massachusetts. (Courtesy of Brian Ballweg/Hofstra.)

Doug Shanahan, 2001. Doug Shanahan was the inaugural winner (2001) of the Tewaaraton Trophy, presented annually to the top lacrosse player in the nation. Shanahan, a three-time All-American, ranks seventh in program history for goals in a single-season (43 in 2001) and ninth in career goals (95). He played on the US National Team and was named MVP of the 2002 World Games. Shanahan was also a four-year starter in the defensive backfield for the football team during his career. (Courtesy of Brian Ballweg/Hofstra.)

CHARLIE ADAMS, 2002. Charlie Adams ranks third all-time in Hofstra history with 2,649 receiving yards. His 1,006 receiving yards in 2000 are the fifth most in a single season at Hofstra. Adams, who played in the NFL with the Denver Broncos, was an All-American in college and the last player at Hofstra to return a punt for a touchdown. He ran the punt back 67 yards against Elon in 2001. (Courtesy of Brian Ballweg/Hofstra.)

STUART DUFFIN, 2000. Stuart Duffin holds the record for career goals and points at Hofstra. He scored 50 goals and recorded 115 points from 1995 to 1999 as a member of the men's soccer team. Duffin was a four-time all-conference selection and America East Player of the Year in 1997, when Hofstra advanced to the America East championship game. (Courtesy of Brian Ballweg/Hofstra.)

Melissa Compton, 1995. Melissa (Compton) Pasko, a dual sport student-athlete in field hockey and women's lacrosse, played for the Pride from 1991 through 1995. During her four-year career on the women's lacrosse team, she scored 94 goals, which ranks 11th all-time, and recorded 123 points. In field hockey she was an all-region selection in 1993, and she was a member of the NFHCA National Academic Team in 1993 and 1994. (Courtesy of Brian Ballweg/Hofstra.)

Dave Fiore, 1996. Dave Fiore was an All-American offensive lineman at Hofstra and spent eight years in the NFL with the San Francisco 49ers and Washington Redskins. At Hofstra, he started 41 of 42 games and helped lead the team to a regular season mark of 28-11-2. In his senior year in 1995, Hofstra was 10-1 during the regular season and advanced to the NCAA I-AA playoffs for the first time. In addition to his All-America selections, he was also named to the All-ECAC team and received the Hempstead Mayor's Trophy. (Courtesy of Brian Ballweg/Hofstra.)

JANET WALSH, 2000. Janet (Walsh) Rogler played women's lacrosse at Hofstra from 1996 to 2000 and is the program's ninth-leading scorer with 101 career goals. She also ranks eighth with 48 career assists and eighth in career points with 149. Walsh was a three-time all-conference selection and an All-American. A member of the field hockey team from 1995 to 1998, Walsh graduated as Hofstra's all-time leader in points with 127 and goals with 55. (Courtesy of Brian Ballweg/Hofstra.)

ERIC SCHMIESING, 2001. One of only nine two-time All-American wrestlers in Hofstra history, Eric Schmiesing achieved the honor in 2000 and 2001 in the 149-pound weight class. Schmiesing, a four-time Academic All-American, ranks third in Hofstra history with 132 career victories. He participated in the NCAA tournament four times and placed fifth in 2000 and eighth in 2001. (Courtesy of Brian Ballweg/Hofstra.)

DIANE HOBIN, 1996. Diane Hobin was one of the most versatile athletes in Hofstra athletics history, competing in three sports—basketball, softball, and field hockey—for the Pride from 1991 to 1996. As a point guard on the Pride basketball team, she scored 1,061 points and added 538 assists and 216 steals in her career. As a member of the softball program, Hobin was a part of NCAA tournament teams in 1993 and 1995 and an ECAC championship team in 1993, and she was also named Hofstra's Outstanding Female Athlete twice during her tenure in Hempstead. (Courtesy of Brian Ballweg/Hofstra.)

HELEEN HILHORST, 1997. An integral part of Hofstra's NCAA tournament volleyball teams in 1995 and 1996, Heleen Hilhorst was named North Atlantic Conference Rookie of the Year in 1994 and Player of the Year in 1995. She is ranked ninth all-time at Hofstra in career kills with 1,122. (Courtesy of Brian Ballweg/Hofstra.)

ROMAN FLESZAR, 2001. Roman Fleszar was a two-time All-American at Hofstra in wrestling and holds the school record for most victories in a season with 44 in 1998–1999. His 130 career victories rank fourth all-time at Hofstra. Fleszar placed seventh and fifth, respectively, at the NCAA tournament in 2000 and 2001. (Courtesy of Brian Ballweg/Hofstra.)

BETH PARR, 1997. Elizabeth (Parr) Parisi played setter and was an important piece of Hofstra's NCAA tournament teams in volleyball in 1995 and 1996. She ranks eighth in matches played (149), fourth in service aces (198), sixth in assists (2,381), and 10th in digs (1,306) in school history. Parr, who also served as an assistant coach for the Pride, dished out 29 assists and had 10 digs against South Carolina in Hofstra's first-ever NCAA tournament match in 1995. (Courtesy Notre Dame Athletics.)

ZAK WRIGHT, 1996. A four-time all-region selection, Zak Wright was a four-year starter for the Hofstra men's soccer team from 1992 through 1995 and left as the Pride's all-time leader in goals (42) and points (96). In 1993, he led Hofstra to a 13-7-1 record, the program's first winning campaign in eight years, and was named the East Coast Conference Player of the Year. He earned ECC Scholar-Athlete of the Year accolades in 1993 and was a 1995 ISAA New York Region Scholar-Athlete first team selection. In 1996, he was named to the CoSIDA Academic All-Region team. (Courtesy of Brian Ballweg/Hofstra.)

Rob Anspach, 2001. Rob Anspach took over as the 11th head coach in Hofstra wrestling history in 2011. As a student-athlete, Anspach compiled a 69-51 record and made two trips to the NCAA championships during his five-year career at Hofstra. As a freshman in 1996–1997, he recorded a 20-13 record and placed third in the ECWA championships. A year later he posted an 18-12 mark, placed third again in the ECWA championships, and captured the New York State Championship title at 167 pounds. (Courtesy of Brian Ballweg/Hofstra.)

Mike Miller, 1995. Mike Miller lettered in baseball at Hofstra from 1992 to 1995. He holds the school record for most home runs in a season with 20 in 1995. He also ranks seventh with 180 hits, second with nine triples, third with 161 RBIs, and first with 167 runs scored. Miller was selected by the Detroit Tigers in the 29th round of the 1995 MLB draft. (Courtesy of Brian Ballweg/Hofstra.)

Raheem Morris, 1998. Raheem Morris was a captain of the football team at Hofstra in 1997, the same year he earned the Mayor's Trophy, presented to a senior football player at the school for good sportsmanship and fair play on and off the field. Morris coached at Hofstra, Cornell, and Kansas State before working his way up the ladder in the Tampa Bay Buccaneers organization, where he became head coach of the Buccaneers in 2009. (Courtesy of Brian Ballweg/Hofstra.)

Simon Riddiough, 1994. Simon Riddiough is the second Hofstra women's soccer coach in school history, taking over from JoAnne Russell at the end of the 2005 season. Riddiough was a four-year letterman and captain of the Flying Dutchmen from 1990 to 1994. In his Hofstra career, he recorded 13 goals and 15 assists. A hard-nosed defender as a player, Riddiough has helped develop the Hofstra women's soccer program into one of the top defensive teams in the nation in recent seasons. (Courtesy of Brian Ballweg/Hofstra.)

Blake Miller, 1996. A two-time US Team player, Blake Miller led the Hofstra lacrosse team in scoring in 1996 with 36 goals. He was named North Atlantic Conference MVP in 1996, the same year he was an All-American. Miller has played on a handful of professional teams in the NLL and MLL. (Courtesy of Brian Ballweg/Hofstra.)

Lance Schulters, 1998. A former All-Pro free safety in the NFL, Lance Schulters was Hofstra's Team MVP and Iron Mike Award winner in 1997. Schulters was a two-time All-American and all-conference selection. The San Francisco 49ers selected him in the fourth round of the 1998 NFL draft. He spent time with San Francisco, Tennessee, Miami, and Atlanta before retiring. Schulters played in the Pro Bowl in 1999 as a member of the 49ers. (Courtesy of University of Delaware.)

ERIN PHILLIPS, 1996. Erin (Phillips) Ortega holds the school record for most strikeouts in a game, striking out 19 against Manhattan in 1996. Phillips, who was part of two NCAA tournament teams and later played professionally in Holland, finished her Hofstra career with 618 strikeouts, ranking her third all-time. She also is ranked fifth with 67 wins and fourth with 667.3 innings pitched. (Courtesy of Brian Ballweg/Hofstra.)

SUZANNE NEWELL, 1998. Suzanne Newell is Hofstra's all-time leading scorer in women's soccer history with 89 points and holds single-game records with four goals and nine points against Central Connecticut in 1996. Newell ranks second all-time at Hofstra with 36 career goals. (Courtesy of Brian Ballweg/Hofstra.)

STEPHANIE CLARKE, 1997. Stephanie Clarke played goalkeeper for the Hofstra women's lacrosse team from 1994 through 1997 and was the first All-American in program history. She recorded a 38-23 record and 909 saves in her four years. In 1996, Clarke helped the Pride to a 13-3 record and a perfect 6-0 mark in the North Atlantic Conference. Hofstra won the NAC championship that season and she was named the tournament's MVP as well as an All-American. Clarke represented her country as a US National Team member. (Courtesy of Brian Ballweg/Hofstra.)

BRIAN LANGTRY, 1998. Brian Langtry ranks 11th in Hofstra men's lacrosse history with 142 career points. He was an All-American and America East Conference MVP in 1998. Langtry's seven goals against Hartford in 1998 are the fourth most in a single game. His 72 points in 1998 are also the seventh most in a single season in school history. Langtry played for multiple teams in the NLL and MLL. (Courtesy of Brian Ballweg/Hofstra.)

LENA MALINOWSKI, 1999. A two-time all-conference selection, Lena Malinowski holds the Hofstra record for kills in volleyball with 1,654 recorded from 1994 to 1998. She also ranks second in digs (1,545) and is tied with one other for the most digs in a contest, recording 41 against Delaware in 1994. Malinowski played on two NCAA tournament teams in 1996 and 1997. (Courtesy of Brian Ballweg/Hofstra.)

TOM PECORA. Tom Pecora was head coach of the Hofstra men's basketball team for nine seasons. He compiled a 155-126 record. From 2004 to 2007, his teams registered three consecutive 20-win seasons and made three straight appearances in the National Invitation Tournament. Pecora joined Hofstra's coaching staff as an assistant in 1994. He has since moved on to coach the men's basketball program at Fordham. (Courtesy of Brian Ballweg/Hofstra.)

JOE AMPLO, 2000. Joe Amplo was a four-year letterman, 1999 All-America East first team selection, and a three-time NCAA championship participant as a lacrosse player at Hofstra. He served on the Pride coaching staff for 11 years and coached in eight more NCAA tournaments, reaching the quarterfinals three times. He became Marquette's first head men's lacrosse coach following the 2011 season. (Courtesy of Brian Ballweg/Hofstra.)

GIOVANNI CARMAZZI, 2000. Giovanni Carmazzi played quarterback on the football team from 1996 to 1999, was a member of two NCAA I-AA playoff teams, and helped the team achieve a No. 5 national ranking in 1999. Hofstra's all-time leader in passing yards with 9,371 and completions with 764, he also holds the school mark for touchdown passes (71) and total offense (10,415 yards). Carmazzi, who was selected in the third round of the 2000 NFL draft by the San Francisco 49ers, was a three-time All-American and a Payton Award finalist as a senior. (Courtesy of Brian Ballweg/Hofstra.)

6

2000s

Craig "Speedy" Claxton, 2000. Speedy Claxton, who led Hofstra to a pair of postseason appearances (1999 NIT and 2000 NCAA tournament), played on the men's basketball team from 1996 to 2000. Claxton, a first round selection in the 2000 NBA draft, finished his career with 2,015 points, 660 assists, and 288 steals. A two-time America East Player of the Year and a Haggerty Award winner, Claxton was a member of the 2003 NBA champion San Antonio Spurs and enjoyed a decade-long NBA career. (Courtesy of Brian Ballweg/Hofstra.)

DANIELLE STEWART, 2003. Danielle (Stewart) Bouman is Hofstra's only Olympic medalist, winning a bronze medal with the Australian National Softball Team at the 2008 Summer Olympics in Beijing, China. Stewart hit two home runs in the Olympics, including one in the bronze medal game. At Hofstra, Stewart was a two-time all-conference selection and holds the record for most home runs in a single season after hitting 17 in 2003. Her 21 home runs rank seventh all-time at Hofstra. She was selected to the Colonial Athletic Association 25th Anniversary Team and played for the Mariners Club in Brisbane, Australia. (Courtesy of Scott Bruhn.)

Alicia Smith, 2000. Hofstra's all-time hits leader in softball with 271, Alicia Smith was an All-American and four-time all-conference selection from 1997 to 2000. Smith also pitched a Hofstra-record 20 innings against Delaware in 2000. She ranks fourth in wins (71), fifth in strikeouts (372), and played professionally for the New York-New Jersey Juggernauts. (Courtesy of Brian Ballweg/Hofstra.)

A-10 Conference Champs, 2001. The Hofstra football team climbed as high as No. 3 in the nation en route to its first Atlantic-10 Conference title in 2001. Hofstra would rank second in the nation in total offense (491.6 yards per game) and fifth in scoring offense (37.9 points per game) as head coach Joe Gardi fielded one of his vintage run-and-shoot teams. Senior receiver Charlie Adams, who played in the NFL, broke the school's career receiving yardage record (2,649) during the memorable campaign. The Pride finished 9-2 overall and lost to Lehigh 27-24 in overtime of the NCAA playoffs. (Courtesy of Brian Ballweg/Hofstra.)

KATHLEEN MIKOWSKI, 2003. Kathleen (Mikowski) Durnin leads the Hofstra women's lacrosse program in career goals (183) and points (240). Her 57 goals in 2003 is a single-season program record, and she ranks second with 148 career ground balls. Mikowski was the America East Conference Rookie of the Year in 2000 and a two-time all-conference and All-America selection. Mikowski also played soccer at Hofstra. (Courtesy of Brian Ballweg/Hofstra.)

RICKY BRYANT, 2004. Ricky Bryant led the Hofstra football team in receptions in 2002 and 2003 and is ranked 13th in program history with both 127 receptions and 1,690 receiving yards. Bryant, a two-time all-conference selection, played with the New England Patriots and San Diego Chargers. (Courtesy of Brian Ballweg/Hofstra.)

TOM KESSLER, 2002. Hofstra's all-time leading goal scorer in men's lacrosse, Tom Kessler finished his career with the Pride with 140 goals. His 51 goals in 2002 are the second highest in a single season in school history. Kessler, who ranks third at Hofstra in career points with 207, was a two-time All-American and played with Baltimore and Bridgeport of the MLL. (Courtesy of Brian Ballweg/Hofstra.)

RICK APODACA, 2003. Rick Apodaca played on two of Hofstra's NCAA tournament teams in men's basketball. He ranks 12th in program history with 1,422 career points and fourth with 190 three-point field goals. Apodaca has played professionally in Puerto Rico, Poland, and Italy. He was on the 2004 Puerto Rican National Basketball Team that defeated the United States in the 2004 Olympic Games. (Courtesy of Brian Ballweg/Hofstra.)

Lisa Ciavardini, 2001. Lisa Ciavardini was an All-American and the 2001 America East Player of the Year in softball at Hofstra. She ranks second in games played in program history (230), fifth in hits (212), second in RBIs (146), fifth in doubles (46), sixth in triples (12), and fifth in walks (80). (Courtesy of Brian Ballweg/Hofstra.)

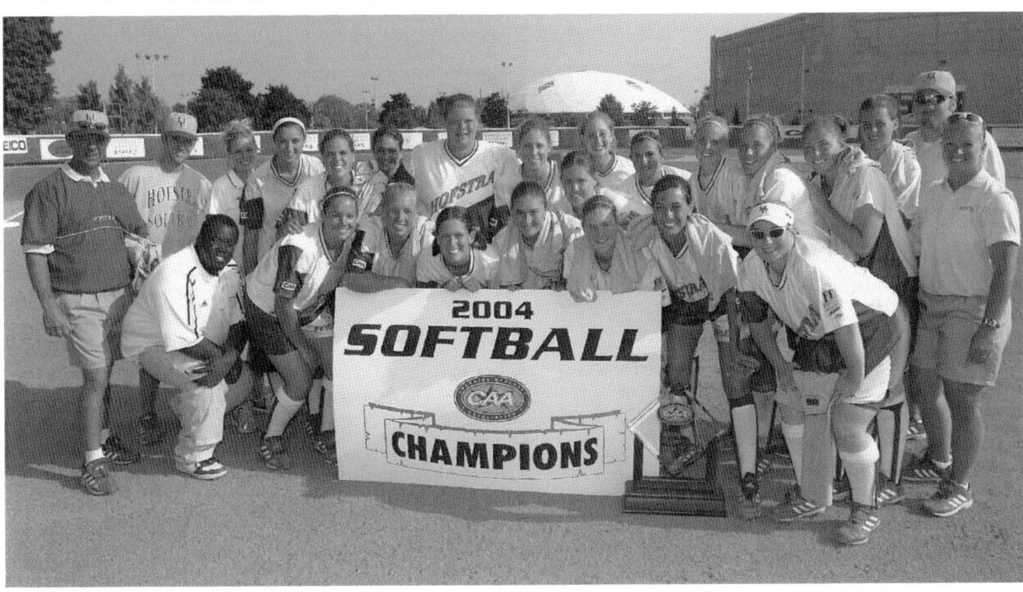

CAA Champions, 2004. In 2004, the Hofstra softball team was one win away from the Women's College World Series. The Pride charged to the NCAA regional finals at Stanford where they won four games, including victories over Auburn and Stanford. Hofstra, which finished 38-21, won the Colonial Athletic Association title and was ranked as high as No. 21 in the nation that season. (Courtesy of Brian Ballweg/Hofstra.)

AMANDA HALLAWAY, 2003. A four-time all-conference selection at Hofstra in softball from 2000 to 2003, Amanda Hallaway was an All-American and a member of the Colonial Athletic Association 25th Anniversary Team. Hallaway, who hit 24 career home runs—a record when she graduated—hit a home run against No. 1 UCLA as a freshman (10-5 win) and a three-run homer at Nebraska as a senior (3-1 win) in the NCAA tournament. Hallaway played on four NCAA tournament teams and ranks fourth in school history with 143 RBIs. (Courtesy of Brian Ballweg/Hofstra.)

ARNI GUNNARSSON, 2004. Arni Gunnarsson was a two-time Academic All-American and two-time all-conference selection in soccer. In 2003, he was named Colonial Athletic Association Scholar-Athlete of the Year. He played professionally in Iceland. (Courtesy of Brian Ballweg/Hofstra.)

KATHLEEN MCPIKE, 2001. Kathleen (McPike) Taylor holds the Hofstra women's lacrosse record for career assists (82) and assists in a season (34 in 2000). McPike, who was a two-time all-conference selection and an All-American, ranks sixth in program history with 124 goals. She also ranks fourth with 206 points, and her 73 points in 2001 are tied for a single-season record at Hofstra. (Courtesy of Brian Ballweg/Hofstra.)

JEN BRICKEY, 2003. Jen Brickey ranks second on the Hofstra women's basketball all-time scoring list with 1,726 points. She played for the Pride from 1999 to 2003. Her 36 points against William & Mary in 2002 are the fourth most in a single game in school history. She also ranks second in program history with 230 three-point shots made. (Courtesy of Brian Ballweg/Hofstra.)

HOFSTRA UNIVERSITY SOCCER STADIUM. Both the men's and women's soccer teams play at the Hofstra University Soccer Stadium, located on the university's north campus. It was constructed in 2003 through a partnership with the New York Jets. It features a 120-yard by 74-yard FieldTurf surface, stadium lighting, press box, metal bleachers the length of the field, and the Gorman Memorial Gateway and the Hofstra Soccer Walls of Honor. The stadium served as the home site of first round NCAA tournament games in 2005 and 2006 and has hosted numerous high school playoff contests. (Courtesy of Brian Ballweg/Hofstra.)

NICKY POLANCO, 2002. Nicky Polanco was a two-time All-American men's lacrosse player at Hofstra. He was named Colonial Athletic Association Defensive Player of the Year and Player of the Year in 2002. Polanco, who has played on multiple teams in the NLL and MLL, was a two-time US World Team player as well. (Courtesy of Brian Ballweg/Hofstra.)

Jen Smith, 2000. One of the most prolific pitchers and hitters in Hofstra softball history, Jen (Smith) Werneke threw five no-hitters and was a two-time America East Pitcher of the Year in 1997 and 1998. In program history, she ranks fourth in strikeouts (600), third in wins (78), fourth in hits (234), and first in appearances (146). Smith was a four-time, all-conference selection and played professionally for the New York-New Jersey Juggernauts. (Courtesy of Brian Ballweg/Hofstra.)

CAA Champions, 2004. The Hofstra men's soccer team had one of its most memorable seasons in 2004, winning a Colonial Athletic Association title as a fifth seed and playing in the NCAA tournament for the first time. The Pride beat nationally ranked Seton Hall 2-1 in the opening round before losing to No. 3 Maryland in the next game. (Courtesy of the Colonial Athletic Association.)

STUART RABINOWITZ. Stuart Rabinowitz, pictured here at the convocation in honor of the university's 75th anniversary, was chosen by the Hofstra University Board of Trustees to serve as the eighth president of the university on December 20, 2000. Prior to his appointment, he served as dean of Hofstra University School of Law from September 1989 through June 2001. He joined the faculty of the Law School in 1972. President Rabinowitz currently holds the Andrew M. Boas and Mark L. Claster Distinguished Professor of Law. (Courtesy of Hofstra University.)

MICHAEL TODD, 2007. Michael Todd earned both All-America and Academic All-America honors as a member of the Hofstra men's soccer team after finishing his career with 101 points. The 2006 CAA Player of the Year, Todd had the game-winning goal in the first two NCAA tournament wins in program history, a 2-1 win over Seton Hall (2004) and a 2-0 win over Providence (2006). (Courtesy of Brian Ballweg/Hofstra.)

JAY WRIGHT. Jay Wright coached the Hofstra men's basketball team for seven seasons (1994–2001), leading the Pride to NCAA tournament appearances in 2000 and 2001. Wright, who left Hofstra with a 122-85 record, earned America East Coach of the Year honors both seasons. He is currently the head men's basketball coach at Villanova. (Courtesy of Brian Ballweg/Hofstra.)

NORMAN RICHARDSON, 2001. Norman Richardson was a member of the men's basketball team at Hofstra from 1997 to 2001. He helped lead Hofstra to back-to-back appearances in the NCAA tournament and won the Haggerty Award in 2001 as the top collegiate basketball player in the New York metropolitan area. Richardson ranks ninth at Hofstra in scoring with 1,677 points and third with 192 three-point field goals made. He was named America East Conference Player of the Year in 2001 and played in the NBA with Indiana and Chicago. (Courtesy of Brian Ballweg/Hofstra.)

Claxton and Richardson in the NBA. This unique photograph features Speedy Claxton (left) and Norman Richardson, two of Hofstra's all-time greats in men's basketball, playing against each other in the NBA. Claxton was with Philadelphia at the time, while Richardson was with Indiana. (Courtesy of Indiana Pacers.)

America East Title Celebration, 2000. Fans mob the court as Hofstra claims its first America East Conference title with a 76-69 victory over Delaware. The victory clinched an NCAA tournament bid for Hofstra, which eventually lost to Oklahoma State in the first round. The Pride finished 24-7 that season. (Courtesy of Howard Gorchov.)

CLAXTON CUTS THE NET. Surrounded by teammates, coaches, and fans, Speedy Claxton rejoices in the moment after cutting down the net following Hofstra's victory over Delaware in the 2000 America East championship game. (Courtesy of Howard Gorchov.)

TEAM FOR THE AGES. The 1999–2000 Hofstra men's basketball team was one of the greatest groups of players in program history. With Speedy Claxton leading the charge and Jay Wright at the helm, Hofstra reached the NCAA tournament for the first time since 1977. The team would advance to another NCAA tournament the following season. (Courtesy of Brian Ballweg/Hofstra.)

TIFFANY YOVINO, 2011. Tiffany Yovino, the 2010 CAA Player of the Year as a senior, helped the Hofstra women's soccer team to a program-best 19-3 record and a spot in the second round of the NCAA tournament. Yovino, who started all 85 games and won more games than any other player in program history (58), was named an All-American, Academic All-American, nominated for NCAA Female Athlete of the Year, and is the school's first recipient of the prestigious NCAA Postgraduate Scholarship. (Courtesy of Alex Trautwig/Hofstra.)

PRIDE UPSET NO. 17 MICHIGAN STATE. During the 2006–2007 season, the first for coach Krista Kilburn-Steveskey, Hofstra captured one of its biggest wins in women's basketball history. Hofstra upset No. 17 Michigan State, 57-53, in its fourth game of the season. The Pride went on to finish 26-8 overall and 13-5 in the Colonial Athletic Association that season. Hofstra has had the good fortune of upsetting other nationally ranked programs in many sports, including three times against No. 1 ranked opponents. The softball team beat UCLA 10-5 in February 2000; the wrestling team upset Minnesota 18-17 in November 2006; and the men's lacrosse team defeated Johns Hopkins in overtime 8-7 in March 2008. (Courtesy of Dave Olds.)

CAA Champions, 2005. In 2005, the Hofstra women's soccer team allowed only three goals in 11 conference games on its way to winning the CAA championship and earning its first-ever NCAA Division I tournament bid. The Pride upset top-seeded Virginia Commonwealth on the road in the conference title game. Hofstra finished 14-4-3 in what was JoAnne Russell's final season as head coach at the university. (Courtesy of the Colonial Athletic Association.)

Antoine Agudio, 2008. The second all-time leading scorer in Hofstra men's basketball history, Antoine Agudio finished his career with 2,276 points. He was a three-time All-Metropolitan selection and holds the school record for three-point field goals in a season with 100 in 2006–2007 and three-point field goals for a career with 357. Agudio played professionally in Turkey and with Albuquerque of the NBDL. (Courtesy of Brian Ballweg/Hofstra.)

BRETT MOYER, 2008. One of the toughest men's lacrosse defenders Hofstra has had in the modern era, Brett Moyer was a three-time All-American and four-time all-conference selection. He was the Colonial Athletic Association Rookie of the Year in 2003 and was a two-time CAA Defensive Player of the Year. Moyer, who was MVP of the North-South All-Star game in 2006, has played for Philadelphia in the NLL and MLL. (Courtesy of Brian Ballweg/Hofstra.)

Charles Griffin, 2008. Charles Griffin wrestled four times in the NCAA tournament, placing third at 141 pounds in both 2007 and 2008. He was a two-time Colonial Athletic Association Wrestler of the Year and two-time All-American. Griffin received the 2008 Howdy Myers Award for best male athlete at Hofstra and finished his career with 126 wins. (Courtesy of Brian Ballweg/Hofstra.)

Bridget Eder, 2005. Bridget Eder played women's lacrosse at Hofstra from 2002 to 2005. She holds the single-season records for ground balls (74 in 2004) and caused turnovers (47 in 2005) and the career records for ground balls (229) and caused turnovers (126). Eder was a two-time All-American, two-time Colonial Athletic Association Defensive Player of the Year, and three-time all-conference selection. In addition, she also earned national defender of the year honors during her career. (Courtesy of Brian Ballweg/Hofstra.)

ADRIENNE CLARK, 2005. Adrienne Clark was a two-time first team All-CAA selection and was named to the NCAA All-Regional team in 2003 and 2004. She developed into one of the top big-game pitchers in the nation, tallying a 5-1 record with one save in NCAA tournament play over her final three seasons, including four wins in 1-0 games. Clark also had a streak of 31 straight shutout innings as a starter in the NCAA tournament. (Courtesy of Brian Ballweg/Hofstra.)

BECKY THORN, 2007. Becky Thorn ranks second in Hofstra women's lacrosse history with 155 career goals. Her 177 points ranks fifth, while her 145 draw controls are first and 127 ground balls are fourth. Thorn was an All-American and three-time all-conference selection, while earning MVP honors at the 2007 CAA championship. (Courtesy of Brian Ballweg/Hofstra.)

CHRIS UNTERSTEIN, 2006. The Colonial Athletic Association Player of the Year in 2006, Chris Unterstein recorded 81 points that season, which is the third highest in school history. He also scored 45 goals that season, the fifth most at Hofstra. Unterstein, who has played for a handful of teams in the MLL, ranks fifth all-time in program history with 166 career points. He was an All-American and won the Howdy Myers Award as the top male athlete at Hofstra in 2006. (Courtesy of Brian Ballweg/Hofstra.)

AARON WEAVER, 2010. Aaron Weaver recorded 135 receptions, 1,416 yards, and eight touchdowns in 26 games during his three-year Hofstra career. The two-time All-CAA second team selection recorded 70 catches for 595 yards as a sophomore and 63 receptions and 797 yards as a junior. Hofstra discontinued its football program after the 2009 season. (Courtesy of Brian Ballweg/Hofstra.)

JAMES M. SHUART STADIUM. Originally known as Hofstra Stadium upon its completion in 1963, its name was changed to honor Dr. James M. Shuart on August 29, 2002. In addition to serving as the home for the Pride men's and women's lacrosse teams, the stadium, which has a seating capacity of 13,000, has served as the location for NCAA championships, county and state high school playoff and championship games for football and lacrosse, world championships for men's and women's lacrosse, professional soccer, commencement exercises, and cultural events. In 1968, it became just the third facility in the country to install an artificial playing surface, following Houston and Indiana State. In 1971, it hosted the first-ever NCAA lacrosse championship between Cornell and Maryland. In 2007, the artificial turf was replaced with FieldTurf. (Courtesy of News 12.)

LAUREN ENGLE, 2009. Lauren Engle was a four-year letter winner on Hofstra's volleyball team and played in the 2006 NCAA tournament with the Pride when the team advanced to the second round. Engle was a 2008 Colonial Athletic Association Scholar-Athlete, the same year she was team MVP. She ranks sixth in school history with 1,255 kills. (Courtesy of Jeff Golden/Hofstra.)

RICKY CAPUTO, 2006. Ricky Caputo played baseball at Hofstra from 2003 to 2006. Along with teammate Josh Stern, Caputo has played in more games than anyone in program history (201). He also ranks second in hits (248), second in home runs (34), fourth in RBIs (160), second in runs (166), and first in triples (10). Caputo was selected in the 24th round of the 2006 MLB draft by the Washington Nationals. (Courtesy of Brian Ballweg/Hofstra.)

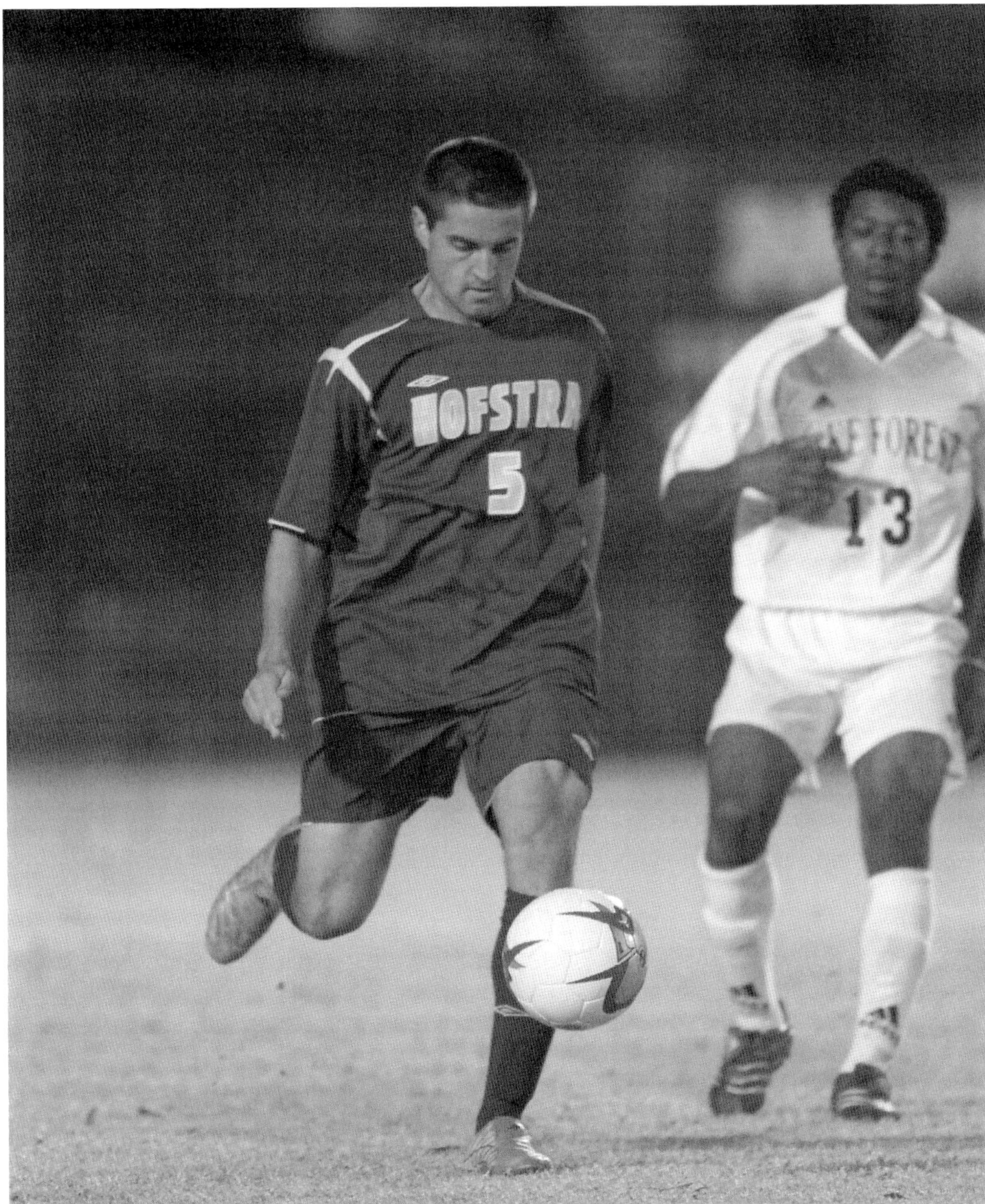

GARY FLOOD, 2007. Gary Flood played in a record 82 games with the Hofstra men's soccer team from 2003 to 2006. He was named the Colonial Athletic Association Tournament Most Outstanding Player in 2005. Flood, a two-time all-conference selection, was drafted by the New England Revolution of the MLS and later played with the Long Island Rough Riders of the USL Premier Development League. (Courtesy of Brian Westerholt/Wake Forest Athletics.)

CHARLIA WARNER, 2008. Charlia Warner played field hockey at Hofstra from 2005 to 2008 and ranks fifth in program history with 105 career points. A three-time all-region selection, Warner scored a then team record 45 points and 20 goals in 2006, the same year she was selected as an All-American. (Courtesy of Brian Ballweg/Hofstra.)

KRISTA KILBURN-STEVESKEY. Krista Kilburn-Steveskey, who was named the 11th head women's basketball coach at Hofstra University on May 16, 2006, took the Pride to the Women's National Invitation Tournament (WNIT) in 2007 and again in 2010. In both of Hofstra's postseason trips, the team advanced to at least the second round, with a trip to the quarterfinals in 2007 and a second round visit in 2010. She has led Hofstra to winning seasons in four of her five years as head coach. (Courtesy of Brian Ballweg/Hofstra.)

JACK HAYES. Jack Hayes was the associate director of athletics at the University of Connecticut before being named Hofstra's eighth athletic director on October 4, 2004. Hayes, a Providence College graduate, reintroduced the Hofstra Athletics Hall of Fame after a 50-year absence and led the effort to retire the uniform numbers of 23 prominent Hofstra student-athletes. In his first seven years, the Pride captured 20 Colonial Athletic Association championships and made 33 postseason appearances, including 25 NCAA tournaments. (Courtesy of Brian Ballweg/Hofstra.)

LOREN STOKES, 2007. Loren Stokes is the fourth all-time leading scorer in Hofstra men's basketball history with 2,148 points. He played in three straight National Invitation Tournaments with the Pride and was the Colonial Athletic Association Player of the Year and an All-American in 2007. Stokes has played professionally in Belgium, Ukraine, and with Erie of the NBDL. (Courtesy of Brian Ballweg/Hofstra.)

SHANTE EVANS, 2013. Shante Evans was the first freshman at Hofstra to lead the women's basketball team in scoring since 1993. Evans, who was named to the Team USA squad for the Pan American Games in 2011, was selected All-CAA first team as a sophomore. She was the first sophomore in program history to reach 1,000 career points, and she entered her junior season ranked 19th in school history. Her 665 rebounds through two seasons are the eighth most in program history. (Courtesy of Joe Rogate/Hofstra.)

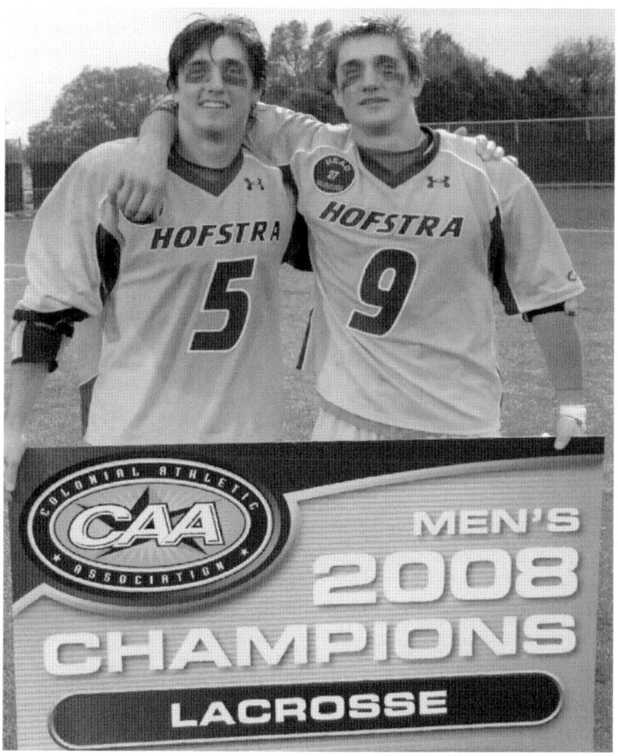

THE UNTERSTEIN BROTHERS, 2008. Kevin and Michael Unterstein, the younger twin brothers of Chris, played on the Hofstra men's lacrosse team for four years. They each played in the North-South All-Star game as seniors. Kevin, currently an assistant men's lacrosse coach at Hofstra, was the CAA Defensive Player of the Year as a senior. As sophomores in 2006, Kevin, his twin brother, Mike, and older brother Chris combined to help lead Hofstra to a 17-2 record, a No. 2 national ranking, and a No. 3 seed in the NCAA tournament. Mike, who is an assistant director of athletic development at Hofstra, was the CAA Rookie of the Year in 2005. (Courtesy of Hofstra University.)

Jersey Numbers Retired. Charles Jenkins, pictured with Mo Cassara, Jack Hayes, and Hofstra president Stuart Rabinowitz, became the 24th Hofstra student-athlete to have a jersey number retired, and the first to earn that distinction while still active when his No. 22 was retired at his final home game on February 26, 2011. The group of retired jerseys, 25 in total, encompasses a wide range of sports and accomplishments as 10 different teams are recognized. Among the honorees are national champions, National Players of the Year, All-Americans, and world champions. (Courtesy of Brian Ballweg/Hofstra.)

CORRINE GANDOLFI, 2010. Corrine Gandolfi was a three-time all-conference selection as a Hofstra women's lacrosse player and started on the 2007 NCAA tournament team. She holds the record with 61 draw controls in a single season and ranks third in career goals (148) and points (209) and is fourth in career assists (61). Gandolfi was a two-time All-American and a member of the US National Team from 2009 to 2011. (Courtesy of David Gonzales/Hofstra.)

BROOKE DEROSA, 2008. Brooke DeRosa made the most of her one season at Hofstra in 2007, when she earned third-team All-America honors. She scored 14 goals on the season for the Pride, including a first-half goal against Penn State in the second round of the NCAA tournament. In Hofstra's CAA semifinal win over James Madison, DeRosa, who transferred from Syracuse, scored a pair of goals to lead the Pride to victory in women's soccer. (Courtesy of Brian Ballweg/Hofstra.)

Hofstra Upsets No. 14 Miami. Hofstra traveled to Miami and beat the No. 14 Hurricanes 5-0 in May 2011 at Alex Rodriguez Park. Pride pitcher David D'Errico (pictured) was named Colonial Athletic Association Pitcher of the Week after throwing six shutout innings and allowing just five hits, all singles, in the win. The victory represented the highest ranked opponent that Hofstra has ever defeated in baseball. Jared Hammer led off the second inning with a double down the right field line and scored when Joe Perez hit a double two batters later to make it 1-0, and it was all the Pride needed to secure the win. Hammer finished 3-for-4 on the day with an RBI and two runs scored, while Perez had two hits and three RBIs. (Courtesy of Jorge Perez/Hofstra.)

EDEL MALONE, 2009. A member of two Hofstra women's soccer teams that played in the NCAA tournament, Edel Malone ranks eighth in school history with 49 career points and 10th with 17 goals. Malone was Colonial Athletic Association Rookie of the Year in 2005. Malone scored the only goal in a 1-0 win over Ohio State in the 2007 NCAA tournament. (Courtesy of Brian Ballweg/Hofstra.)

ETHAN PAQUETTE, 2010. In 2010, Ethan Paquette set a Hofstra baseball single-season record with 70 RBIs. He also recorded 76 hits and 14 home runs, both ranking him third all-time in single-season history. That same year he was selected by the Seattle Mariners in the 35th round of the MLB draft. (Courtesy of Brian Ballweg/Hofstra.)

Athan Iannucci, 2006. Athan Iannucci set the Hofstra men's lacrosse single-season scoring record with 62 goals in 2006. His 104 career goals rank eighth in school history, and his 146 career points ranks ninth. Iannucci, an All-American in 2006, has played for Toronto and Chicago in the MLL and was NLL MVP in 2008 while playing for Philadelphia. In his second season in the NLL, he broke Gary Gait's record of 61 goals in a season, finishing with 71 in 2008. (Courtesy of Brian Ballweg/Hofstra.)

GENNA KOVAR, 2012. Genna Kovar ranks as the top offensive field hockey player in Hofstra history. A two-time NFHCA All-American, a three-time All-Mideast Region selection, and a three-time All-CAA first team pick, she had a record-breaking senior season, setting the Hofstra mark for goals, assists, and points. In the process, she also set records for career goals, assists, and points. Kovar capped her career by being named to the NFHCA Senior All-Star Game. (Courtesy of Ben Solomon/Hofstra.)

JESS CRANKSHAW, 2009. A three-time all-conference selection in women's soccer, Jess Crankshaw was the Colonial Athletic Association Defensive Player of the Year in 2008 while playing for the Pride. She also earned NSCAA Scholar All-America honors in 2008. (Courtesy of Joe Rokita/Hofstra.)

Marques Colston, 2006. Marques Colston is the second all-time leading receiver in Hofstra football history with 2,834 yards. He also caught the third-most passes in school history (182) and holds the record for most receiving yards in a game (276 versus Liberty in 2003). Colston was selected by the New Orleans Saints in the seventh round of the 2006 NFL draft, winning a Super Bowl title with the Saints in 2009. (Courtesy of University of Delaware.)

Lizanne Murphy, 2007. Lizanne Murphy played women's basketball at Hofstra from 2003 to 2007. She finished her career as the 12th all-time leading scorer in program history with 1,245 points. Murphy also ranks second at Hofstra with 988 career rebounds. In Hofstra's upset of South Carolina in the 2007 WNIT, Murphy led the Pride with a game-high 18 points. (Courtesy of Brian Ballweg/Hofstra.)

DAVID S. MACK SPORTS AND EXHIBITION COMPLEX. The Mack Sports Complex is a $15-million, 93,000-square-foot facility that was completed in December 1999. It was originally known as Hofstra Arena and renamed the David S. Mack Sports and Exhibition Complex in 2006. Aside from playing host to men's basketball championships and NIT contests—and featuring wins over teams from the Big East, Big 12, and Atlantic 10 conferences as well as wins in the Women's NIT—and numerous wrestling matches over ranked opponents, the arena also featured the third and final debate between presidential candidates Barack Obama and John McCain, which was broadcast live around the world. In 2010, the Mack Sports Complex hosted NBC Late Night talk show host Jimmy Fallon as part of the university's 75th anniversary celebration. (Courtesy of Chris R. Vaccaro.)

BRITTANY BUTTS, 2011. Brittany Butts earned first team All-CAA honors as Hofstra's 2010 women's soccer team broke school records for the most wins in a season (19), most consecutive wins (18), and most conference wins (11). The 18 straight victories tied for the third-longest winning streak in Hofstra history in any sport. During the 2010 campaign, Butts played an important role in wins over Indiana, Purdue, and Connecticut (NCAA tournament), including scoring a goal against the Hoosiers. (Courtesy of Brian Ballweg/Hofstra.)

KATIE HERTSCH, 2011. A two-time all-conference selection in women's lacrosse, Katie Hertsch finished her Hofstra career with 138 ground balls (third all-time), 70 caused turnovers (fifth), and 110 draw controls (fifth). Since 2009, Hertsch has been a part of the US National Lacrosse program. (Courtesy of Brian Ballweg/Hofstra.)

FROM HOFSTRA TO THE NFL. This photograph was taken at a press conference at Margiotta Hall in 2006 when three Hofstra football players officially began a new chapter in their lives. Stephen Bowen (left) signed with the Dallas Cowboys, while Willie Colon (center) was drafted by the Pittsburgh Steelers, and Marques Colston (right) was drafted by the New Orleans Saints. (Courtesy of Chris R. Vaccaro.)

KAYLEIGH LOTTI, 2009. A four-time all-conference selection, Kayleigh Lotti holds the Hofstra softball record for career strikeouts with 979. She threw four no-hitters, recorded 82 wins, and was a three-time Colonial Athletic Association Pitcher of the Year during her four-year career, which lasted from 2006 to 2009. (Courtesy of Brian Ballweg/Hofstra.)

NIKOLA DJORDJEVIC, 2006. Nikola Djordjevic was the Colonial Athletic Association Rookie of the Year in tennis in 2003. He was honored with the Dr. James M. Shuart Award three times as the top male athlete in recognition of achievement in academics. Djordjevic was also an all-conference selection and two-time Academic All-American recipient. (Courtesy of Brian Ballweg/Hofstra.)

CHRIS SKRETKOWICZ, 2005. Chris Skretkowicz, who wrestled four times at the NCAA championships, earned All-American honors by placing sixth in 2003 and fifth in 2004. He was a two-time Colonial Athletic Association Wrestler of the Year in 2003 and 2004 and Colonial Athletic Association Rookie of the Year in 2002. His 140 wins are the most in Hofstra wrestling history. (Courtesy of Brian Ballweg/Hofstra.)

THE HOFSTRA SEAL. The Hofstra seal was designed from the royal Dutch emblem by art instructor Constant Van de Wall. The seal carries the motto of the House of Orange-Nassau in Old French: *Je maintiendray* ("I stand steadfast"). The Hofstra seal is still in use today, not as a logo but it is used on formal documents. The first consistent use of the word "Pride" relating to athletics was in 1989 when the university's athletic booster club was founded and called itself The Pride Club. (Courtesy of Hofstra University.)

HOFSTRA'S CURRENT ATHLETIC LOGO. Hofstra's athletic teams are officially known as the Pride, providing teams with a strong, consistent image that resonates with the Hofstra community. The new Hofstra athletics logo, developed in 2005, consists of a graphic mark of a male and female lion in powerful, synchronized motion with the word mark of the Hofstra Pride or the specific sports team. (Courtesy of Hofstra University.)

Kim Hillier, 2007. Kim Hillier was a four-time all-conference selection as a women's lacrosse player at Hofstra. She finished her career second in school history with 215 points and fourth with 133 goals. Hillier, who was the Colonial Athletic Association Rookie of the Year in 2004, also played for the US National Team. (Courtesy of Brian Ballweg/Hofstra.)

Shaun Foster, 2014. Shaun Foster was the first player in CAA men's soccer history to win two major awards in the same season when he earned Rookie of the Year and Defensive Player of the Year honors in 2010. In addition to his two major awards, Foster was chosen to the All-CAA first team, the only freshman to earn that accolade. (Courtesy of Brian Ballweg/Hofstra.)

ELIZABETH CURLEY, 2007. Elizabeth (Curley) Messmer played volleyball at Hofstra from 2003 to 2006. In that time she earned two all-conference selections, Colonial Athletic Association Rookie of the Year honors in 2003, Player of the Year honors in 2006, and she was named the Nassau County Sports Commission College Athlete of the Year in 2007. Curley was also an American Volleyball Coaches Association All-American (the only one in program history) and selected to the Colonial Athletic Association 25th Anniversary Team. She was on Hofstra's 2006 NCAA tournament team and finished her career ranked fourth in school history in total blocks with 453 and seventh in kills with 1,160. (Courtesy of Joe Rokita/Hofstra.)

VANESSA GIDDEN, 2007. Vanessa Gidden played women's basketball at Hofstra from 2003 to 2007. She ended her Hofstra career ranked seventh all-time at the school in scoring (1,489), third in rebounds (911), and second in shots blocked (175). Gidden scored 12 points against Michigan State in an upset of the No. 17 Spartans during the 2006–2007 season. (Courtesy of Brian Ballweg/Hofstra.)

WILLIE COLON, 2006. Willie Colon won the Iron Mike Award as the MVP of Hofstra's football team in 2005. The following spring he was selected by the Pittsburgh Steelers in the fourth round of the 2006 NFL draft. Colon, an offensive tackle, won a Super Bowl with the Steelers in 2008. (Courtesy of Marshall University.)

SHELLANE OGOSHI, 2008. Shellane Ogoshi finished her distinguished playing career in 2007, during which she accumulated 4,597 assists and 1,660 digs and currently holds the top spot in program history in both categories. The 2004 CAA Rookie of the Year, the 2005 CAA Player of the Year, and the 2005 and 2006 CAA Setter of the Year, Ogoshi helped lead Hofstra to the second round of the NCAA tournament in 2006 for the first time in program history. Ogoshi is currently the head volleyball coach at LIU-CW Post. (Courtesy of Brian Ballweg/Hofstra.)

SETH TIERNEY. Seth Tierney was named the fifth men's lacrosse head coach in school history following the 2006 season. Tierney, who served as a Pride assistant from 1995 through 2000, has recorded a school record four consecutive NCAA championship appearances as head coach. Entering the 2012 season, he owns the highest winning percentage (.653) by a Hofstra men's lacrosse coach. (Courtesy of Brian Ballweg/Hofstra.)

KRISTA THORN, 2012. Krista Thorn became the first Hofstra female student-athlete to participate in NCAA tournaments in two different sports when she helped the women's soccer and softball teams earn bids in 2010. She also helped both programs to their winningest seasons in the process (45-12 with softball and 19-3 with women's soccer). Thorn, a goalkeeper, also plays soccer for the Long Island Lady Rough Riders. (Courtesy of Brian Ballweg/Hofstra.)

Phil Giackette, 2011. Phil Giackette ran cross country at Hofstra for four years, from 2007 to 2010. He holds the second fastest 8K time with a mark of 25:27 in 2009. Giackette also ran the sixth fastest time in school history in the 10K (32:49) at the 2010 NCAA regionals and ran 16:00, a school record, at the 5K Hofstra Invitational in 2009. (Courtesy of Brian Ballweg/Hofstra.)

Cigi McCollin, 2007. Cigi McCollin played women's basketball at Hofstra from 2002 to 2007. She is the fourth all-time leading scorer in school history with 1,662 points. McCollin, who ranks first in program history in games played (126) and in three-point field goals made (291), scored 24 points against No. 17 Michigan State in a stunning upset during the 2006–2007 season. (Courtesy of Brian Ballweg/Hofstra.)

Mike Patrovich, 2007. A four-time NCAA qualifier and two-time All-American in wrestling, Mike Patrovich placed twice in the NCAA tournament during his career at Hofstra. In 2006, he finished fourth and followed that with a sixth-place finish in 2007. Patrovich was named Colonial Athletic Association Wrestler of the Year in 2006 and was selected to the Colonial Athletic Association 25th Anniversary Team. (Courtesy of Brian Ballweg/Hofstra.)

Mary Sullivan, 2009. Mary Sullivan was named 2005 Colonial Athletic Association Rookie of the Year in cross country and continued to impress throughout her career. Sullivan holds the school record in the 5K with a time of 17:58 and a school record in the 6K (21:11), set at the CAA championships in 2005. (Courtesy of Brian Ballweg/Hofstra.)

Nick Colleluori. Nick Colleluori was a lacrosse player for Hofstra. In his sophomore year, he was diagnosed with non-Hodgkin's lymphoma, a type of blood cancer that affects the lymphatic system. Colleluori passed away on November 28, 2006, at the age of 21. His name lives on in the HEADstrong Foundation, which he founded to raise cancer awareness. In 2008, the Hofstra Athletics Department renamed the Pride's Unsung Hero Award, which was established in 2007, in memory of Colleluori. (Courtesy of Jim Sheehan/Hofstra.)

Becky Wachsberger, 2006. Becky Wachsberger graduated from Hofstra having recorded more saves (302) than anyone in the history of the women's soccer program. She was the starting goalkeeper on Hofstra's 2005 NCAA tournament team. Wachsberger played at Hofstra from 2001 to 2005 and was a three-time all-conference selection. (Courtesy of Brian Ballweg/Hofstra.)

ASHLEY LANE, 2007. Ashley Lane played on four NCAA tournament teams while a member of the softball team at Hofstra. She was a four-time all-conference selection and earned Colonial Athletic Association Rookie of the Year honors in 2004 and Player of the Year honors in 2006. Lane is in the Hofstra record books for various career marks, including third in career hits (240), first in home runs (40), second in doubles (54), first in RBIs (180), second in walks (102), and third in at-bats (683). (Courtesy of Brian Ballweg/Hofstra.)

CHRISSY ARNONE, 2006. Chrissy Arnone began her Hofstra women's soccer career as a walk-on and finished it as an Academic All-American. Arnone, currently an assistant director of athletics at Hofstra, was the leading scorer of the first Pride women's soccer team to reach the NCAA tournament (2005). In the 2005 CAA championship, Arnone scored the game-winning goal in the semifinals and assisted on the game-winning goal in the title game. (Courtesy of Brian Ballweg/Hofstra.)

MATT PROKOPOWICZ, 2010. As a freshman in 2007, Matt Prokopowicz recorded a program record 82 hits with the Hofstra baseball team and earned Colonial Athletic Association Rookie of the Year honors. Prokopowicz went on to be a two-time all-conference selection and set the record for the most hits in Hofstra history with 271. (Courtesy of Ross Obley/Hofstra.)

JON MASA, 2006. Jon Masa is Hofstra's only three-time All-America wrestler. He qualified for the NCAA tournament four times, placing seventh in 2003, third in 2005, and fifth in 2006. Masa, who ranks sixth at Hofstra with 126 career victories, was named the 2005 Colonial Athletic Association Wrestler of the Year. (Courtesy of Brian Ballweg/Hofstra.)

Richard Martinez, 2011. Richard Martinez was a three-time all-conference selection as a defender on the Hofstra men's soccer team. He won Colonial Athletic Association Defensive Player of the Year honors in 2009. Martinez has also played for the Puerto Rican National Team. (Courtesy of Brian Ballweg/Hofstra.)

Tom Ryan. Tom Ryan coached the wrestling team at Hofstra from 1995 to 2006, recording 109 dual match victories. In that time, the Pride won six straight conference titles and he was named conference coach of the year seven times. Ryan coached numerous wrestlers who won conference championships and competed at the NCAA tournament. He is currently the head wrestling coach at Ohio State. (Courtesy of Brian Ballweg/Hofstra.)

CASEY MCGRATH, 2007. Casey McGrath played on the Hofstra women's lacrosse team for four years and as a senior helped lead the Pride to the NCAA tournament. McGrath was a three-time all-conference selection and finished fifth in Hofstra history with 125 goals and sixth with 162 points. (Courtesy of Northwestern University.)

DONI-MELISSA JANTZEN, 2007. A two-time All-American, Doni-Melissa Jantzen finished her career with the Hofstra field hockey team as the 10th all-time leading scorer with 18 goals. Jantzen was also a three-time all-conference selection. (Courtesy of Brian Ballweg/Hofstra.)

Mo Cassara. Mo Cassara took over the Hofstra men's basketball helm in 2010, guiding the Pride to a 21-12 overall record and a 14-4 conference mark in his first season. The 21 wins were the most for a first-year head coach of the program since Paul Lynner won 23 games in 1962–1963, and the 14 CAA wins matched the highest total since joining the league in 2001–2002. (Courtesy of Brian Ballweg/Hofstra.)

Olivia Galati, 2013. As a freshman, Olivia Galati was Hofstra's No. 1 pitcher. She took home Colonial Athletic Association Pitcher of the Year and Rookie of the Year honors in 2010, along with earning first team All-CAA, first team NFCA All-Northeast Region, and CAA Tournament Most Outstanding Player honors. As a sophomore in 2011, Galati was the CAA Pitcher of the Year and set the school single-season victory (29), strikeout (348), and shutout (17) records. (Courtesy of Brian Ballweg/Hofstra.)

SUE WEBER, 2008. Sue (Weber) Alber was a three-time Colonial Athletic Association Defensive Player of the Year in women's soccer at Hofstra and a two-time All-American. Weber played on Hofstra's NCAA tournament teams in 2005 and 2007 and was a two-time CAA Scholar Athlete of the Year. She played professionally with the Boston Breakers of Women's Professional Soccer and was the Women's League Defender of the Year with the Long Island Riders in 2008 and 2010. During her career at Hofstra, she played every minute of every game. (Courtesy of Joe Rokita/Hofstra.)

CHARLES JENKINS, 2010. One of the greatest players in Hofstra men's basketball history, Charles Jenkins was selected by the Golden State Warriors in the second round of the 2011 NBA draft. He graduated as Hofstra's all-time leading scorer with 2,513 points, ranking him second in Colonial Athletic Association history behind only David Robinson of Navy. Jenkins also became only the third player to win the Haggerty Award as the top player in the New York metropolitan area three times. Jenkins also was a two-time CAA Player of the Year and earned third-team All-America honors. In addition to holding the Hofstra scoring, games played (128), field goals made (847), and free throws made (639) records, he also ranks fifth in school history in assists (489), steals (213), and three-pointers (177). He is one of only two players, along with Speedy Claxton, to finish with at least 2,000 points, 500 rebounds, and 400 assists. (Courtesy of Jeff Jacobsen/Hofstra.)

JAY CARD, 2011. A three-time All-American, Jay Card was the 2009 CAA Player of the Year for men's lacrosse and 2008 CAA Rookie of the Year. Card, who led Hofstra to a school record four straight NCAA tournament appearances, concluded his career ranked second in goals (122), fifth in points (182), and 11th in assists (60) on Hofstra career charts. A four-time All-CAA selection, Card scored the game-winner in overtime when Hofstra took down top-ranked Johns Hopkins in 2008. (Courtesy of Darl Zehr/Hofstra.)

Discover Thousands of Local History Books Featuring Millions of Vintage Images

Arcadia Publishing, the leading local history publisher in the United States, is committed to making history accessible and meaningful through publishing books that celebrate and preserve the heritage of America's people and places.

Find more books like this at
www.arcadiapublishing.com

Search for your hometown history, your old stomping grounds, and even your favorite sports team.

Consistent with our mission to preserve history on a local level, this book was printed in South Carolina on American-made paper and manufactured entirely in the United States. Products carrying the accredited Forest Stewardship Council (FSC) label are printed on 100 percent FSC-certified paper.

MADE IN THE USA